The English–Vernacular Divide

BILINGUAL EDUCATION AND BILINGUALISM

Series Editors: Professor Colin Baker, *University of Wales, Bangor, Wales, Great Britain* and Professor Nancy H. Hornberger, *University of Pennsylvania, Philadelphia, USA*

Recent Books in the Series

Language Use in Interlingual Families: A Japanese-English Sociolinguistic Study
  Masayo Yamamoto
Cross-linguistic Influence in Third Language Acquisition
  J. Cenoz, B. Hufeisen and U. Jessner (eds)
Learners' Experiences of Immersion Education: Case Studies of French and Chinese
  Michèle de Courcy
Language Minority Students in the Mainstream Classroom (2nd edn)
  Angela L. Carrasquillo and Vivian Rodríguez
World English: A Study of its Development
  Janina Brutt-Griffler
Power, Prestige and Bilingualism: International Perspectives on Elite Bilingual Education
  Anne-Marie de Mejía
Identity and the English Language Learner
  Elaine Mellen Day
Language and Literacy Teaching for Indigenous Education: A Bilingual Approach
  Norbert Francis and Jon Reyhner
The Native Speaker: Myth and Reality
  Alan Davies
Language Socialization in Bilingual and Multilingual Societies
  Robert Bayley and Sandra R. Schecter (eds)
Language Rights and the Law in the United States: Finding our Voices
  Sandra Del Valle
Continua of Biliteracy: An Ecological Framework for Educational Policy, Research, and Practice in Multilingual Settings
  Nancy H. Hornberger (ed.)
Languages in America: A Pluralist View (2nd Edition)
  Susan J. Dicker
Trilingualism in Family, School and Community
  Charlotte Hoffmann and Jehannes Ytsma (eds)
Multilingual Classroom Ecologies
  Angela Creese and Peter Martin (eds)
Negotiation of Identities in Multilingual Contexts
  Aneta Pavlenko and Adrian Blackledge (eds)
Beyond the Beginnings: Literacy Interventions for Upper Elementary English Language Learners
  Angela Carrasquillo, Stephen B. Kucer and Ruth Abrams
Bilingualism and Language Pedagogy
  Janina Brutt-Griffler and Manka Varghese (eds)
Language Learning and Teacher Education: A Sociocultural Approach
  Margaret R. Hawkins (ed.)

For more details of these or any other of our publications, please contact:
Multilingual Matters, Frankfurt Lodge, Clevedon Hall,
Victoria Road, Clevedon, BS21 7HH, England
http://www.multilingual-matters.com

BILINGUAL EDUCATION AND BILINGUALISM 49
Series Editors: Colin Baker and Nancy H. Hornberger

The English-Vernacular Divide
Postcolonial Language Politics and Practice

Vaidehi Ramanathan

MULTILINGUAL MATTERS LTD
Clevedon • Buffalo • Toronto

Library of Congress Cataloging in Publication Data
Ramanathan, Vaidehi
The English-Vernacular Divide: Postcolonial Language Politics and Practice
Vaidehi Ramanathan.
Includes bibliographical references and index.
1. English language–Commonwealth countries. 2. English language–Political
aspects–Commonwealth countries. 3. English language–Social
aspects–Commonwealth countries. 4. English language–Variation–Commonwealth
countries. 5. Languages in contact–Commonwealth countries. 6.
Postcolonialism–Commonwealth countries. 7. Commonwealth countries–Languages.
I. Title.
PE2751.R36 2004
420'.9171241–dc22   2004002831

British Library Cataloguing in Publication Data
A catalogue entry for this book is available from the British Library.

ISBN 1-85359-770-8 (hbk)
ISBN 1-85359-769-4 (pbk)

Multilingual Matters Ltd
UK: Frankfurt Lodge, Clevedon Hall, Victoria Road, Clevedon BS21 7HH.
USA: UTP, 2250 Military Road, Tonawanda, NY 14150, USA.
Canada: UTP, 5201 Dufferin Street, North York, Ontario M3H 5T8, Canada.

Copyright © 2005 Vaidehi Ramanathan.

Typeset by Patrick Armstrong Book Production Services.
Printed and bound in Great Britain by the Cromwell Press Ltd.

Contents

Preface

This intermixture of the Indian languages and English...is not a mirage: by now, after nearly two centuries of continuous aesthetic refinement, the highly crafted 'English' of Indian-English literature is full of the long shadows of Indian languages. The indigenous languages are some among the social, political, and aesthetic elements that have penetrated the English language in its alien environment on the subcontinent, and like other precolonial and noncolonial presences, they have leaked continuously into this literature through the aperture that opened inside two hundred years ago....this shadowy interspersion constitutes a pervasive, internal 'decolonization' of English at the level of language itself. And, in the logic of intercultural contestation and 'post'-colonialism, that – perhaps – is exactly as it should be. (Dharwadkar, 2003: 262)

As scholars in World Englishes have long been testitfying (e.g. Kachru, 1997; Smith & Forman, 1997), English in postcolonial communities is a splintered, hybrid English, being appropriated, nativized and adapted by local environments (Canagarajah, 1999a). Within this already fractured scene, though, exist splits and it is particular English-related divides as they occur in one particular postcolonial context (namely India) that is at the heart of this book. English, as the ensuing pages demonstrate, is entrenched in the heart of a class-based divide (with ancillary ones of gender and caste as well) and issues of inequality, subordination and unequal value seem to revolve directly around its general positioning with Vernacular languages. This issue of English – access to it, being fluent in it, 'moving up' in the world because of it – playing a divisive role on the postcolonial ground has generally remained unarticulated. The English that I speak of in this book is Indian/South-Asian English: I am proceeding from the assumption that it is its own variety and has to be understood as such with subtle shadings and nuances of its own and not as a variety that should be compared to 'native-speaking varieties of English'. As the quote from Dharwadkar (2003: 262) points out, English has cast 'long shadows' for more than a couple of centuries on the subcontinent constituting a 'decolonizing' at the 'level of language itself'. Postcolonial hybridity – of the sort on which the book is based – by its nature implies nativizing; i.e.

appropriating the colonizer's language (in this case, English) to fit and reflect local ways of thinking, knowing, behaving, acting and reasoning in the world. In some instances, the contexts of appropriation are fraught with tension, producing instances of outright rejection or mockery. In other contexts, the appropriation 'seems' relatively 'seamless'. Regardless, though, appropriation and nativization are the default in such contexts, occupying different points on several co-existing biliteracy continua that makes room for both gradual development and occasional back-tracking (Hornberger, 2003), and it is on this hybrid *continuous* ground that the present searching is to be understood. Indeed, as some of the chapters will point out (specifically Chapters 3 and 6), 'localizing' and 'nativizing' occupy different points of several intersecting literacy continua, being more or less obvious in the relatively divergent 'Vernacular-medium' and 'English-medium' settings.

The issue of how language policies at all levels – nation-wide, state-wide, institutional – impact schooling-related domains on such hybrid continuous grounds is central to the book as well. While the book is not about issues in language policy and planning *per se*, it is about the ways in which students, teachers and institutions interpret and engage with particular language policies to build bridges across perceived chasms, while respecting tensions in contact zones. Much of the scholarship in language policy and planning (e.g. Baker, 2000; Bauldauf & Luke, 1990; Cummins, 1988, 2000; Hornberger, 2003; Spolsky, 1986; Tollefson, 1995; Martin-Jones & Jones, 2000; May, 2001) has already paved the way for the 'situated' understanding of language policies undertaken here. Indeed, along with research in other bi/multilingual realms (Baker [2003] in the context of Wales; Bloch and Alexander [2003] in the context of South African schools and Mercado [2003] in the context of Latino youths in New York), the present exploration offers glimpses into some of the complex ways in which language policies around bi/multilingualism get connected to 'local' facets on the ground; i.e. how language policies become social practices; how they are interpreted and resisted by teachers and institutions; how they connect to larger political ideologies; and how they reinforce existing social stratifications. In other words, the book views *language policies as hybrid entities* in themselves, drawing their force and movement from the lives of real peoples and their motivations.

While this notion of hybridity is the general default of this book, certain dichotomies do exist and while that might seem contradictory at first glance (how can one ascribe to the fluid/hybrid nature of all beings, while also adopting a more generalized view?), it is, in fact, not that incongruous at all. Postmodern views of cultures and peoples as being fluid and

dynamic and of all identities being hybrid are most valuable, most especially because they give us a way of talking about individuals in contexts.
But social stratifications of class, caste, ethnicity and gender in societies
still exist and when languages – especially English and the Vernaculars in
postcolonial contexts – seem to fall along those lines, then a critically and
ethnographically oriented researcher has little choice but to address the
chasms as well. In this sense, then, the book contributes to the larger globalization and English narrative by singling out instances of divides lying
latent beneath contexts of appropriation. Synthetic as the yoking of
hybridity and stratification may seem, it is a yoking that I have deliberately chosen to construct, since it is the only one that to me (right now)
seems comprehensive and honest. So, over and above the contact zones in
which the learners, teachers, institutions and I find ourselves, this book
carves out yet another one, namely one in 'research' orientation and
methods: I situate this book squarely in the centre of both hybridism and
chasms, fluidity and fixed points. Paradoxical as it may seem, they are not
necessarily mutually exclusive. Yet another tension in the 'researching'
aspect of this exploration deserves mention, namely conflicts between
capturing the dynamic fluid aspects of reality, including numerous voices
and my own vacillating role as insider and outsider, in the mummified,
frozen genres of writing. Because I am writing about fellow human beings
– indeed, fellow Indians – questioning, thinking and participating in their
everyday teaching and learning domains, I have felt, time and again, that
the genres oriented to 'empirically-oriented' explorations fall short: they
do not, by any means, even begin to capture the myriad, contradictory
ways in which gulfs and bridges get noticed and overcome. Yet, I am
drawing on these genres because they are the venues through which my
writing is most likely to reach readers. As I explain in some detail in the
Introduction, these and other clashing strains inform most aspects of this
piece of work.

As will be apparent, I write here of several chasms in the complex
socio-educational landscape that raised and schooled me, including the
crucial one of 'English-medium' (EM) and 'Vernacular-medium' (VM)
(Tollefson & Tsui, 2004). Partially constituted by colonial legacy and postcolonial practice, this gulf pits students educated in the VM in unequal
opposition to those educated in the EM in India. As one schooled in the
EM, I, in this exploration, partially understand how college-going VM
students get positioned in the English–Vernacular divide and the ways in
which they and their teachers negotiate the relative importance accorded
to English in their lives. While I intuitively and intellectually sensed that
their journeys were quite different from mine and others like me, it was

not until I actually began my forays into the VM worlds that I realized the extent and depth of certain chasms. The metaphor of gulfs and bridges that I use throughout the book, then, needs to be understood against an overall backdrop of an amalgam of sustained splintering and unceasing contact.

The explorations offered in this book represent several conflicting sentiments that have stayed with me through the researching process. The discursive act of writing, where, for the sake of coherence and argument, I have selectively held up some facets for scrutiny, seems to belie the plurality of the context. I realize that this is a troubling issue that is going to continue to plague researchers that do this kind of research. Another difficult issue has to do with my speaking for students and teachers in the VM. As one raised in and bred in the EM track of the Indian educational system, I ask myself constantly if I can speak for a group of learners and teachers whose experiences were, in many ways, quite different from my own. While these questions have pestered me all along, the key issue that has kept me focused on the project has been the overwhelming support I have received from all (EM and VM) people engaged in teaching VM students and from the VM students themselves. Unequivocally, these people have maintained that the wide gap between the two mediums – set in place – from the kindergarten to the 12th grade level – is one that is seldom seriously and critically addressed at the tertiary level. Change, slow and gradual as it is in all educational systems, starts with an analytic consciousness of problems in the first place and, for me, the present endeavor represents early steps toward addressing some realities regarding the divisive role of English on the Indian postcolonial ground. So it is with mixed emotions that I present this to the Applied Linguistics/TESOL worlds. I have tried, as much as possible, to walk the fine line between being a 'researcher' and 'native' and I cannot really tell if I have succeeded. And I suppose, in the end, it does not really matter, except to the (VM) students, teachers and administrators since it is they who gave unstintingly of their time and energy.

Very many people have helped me over these seven years with this endeavor – students, faculty, administrators, former deans and supervisors. Several went out of their way to call my attention to finer points in the educational machinery. I especially thank Father Francis Parmar, S.J., Father Vincent Saldana, S.J., Father Vincent Braganza, S.J., Arati Kumar, Rohini Mokashi-Punekar, Rita Kothari, Sarvar Sherry Chand and Suguna Ramanathan at the Jesuit institution for their unwavering support about all issues Vernacular. At the business college, Havovi Trivedi helped me to see how English, the Vernaculars, disciplines and class simultaneously inform aspects of language teaching and learning, while Chirag Trivedi, himself schooled in the Vernacular, works to build bridges for VM students in this (EM) setting. Mr D.B. Pandya, Tarlaben Desai, Mr T.J. Purani and Kinjal Desai at the women's college spent long hours with me in empty classrooms in the women's college explaining to me their local struggles against the English–Vernacular gulf, both in and out of the classroom. The EM and VM students at all three colleges sacrificed many of their free periods talking to me and showing me their notes. Dinkar Trivedi and Vijay Sherry Chand – neither of whom are affiliated with the institutions described here but who have worked for years in Vernacular-related educational realms – helped enormously by helping me piece together the political background of English and the Vernaculars in Gujarat. Suguna Ramanathan and Sarvar Sherry Chand, who have spent years in the English–Vernacular trenches in Ahmedabad, have given me nuanced feedback each time I have sought it.

My conversations with colleagues and students – especially Dwight Atkinson, John Hedgcock, Brian Morgan, Alastair Pennycook, Suresh Canagarajah, Mary Schleppegrell, Paul McPherron and Jason Schneider – continue to influence my thinking about language teaching and critical practice. I am especially grateful to Suresh Canagarajah, who gave me detailed and most valuable comments on the entire manuscript. His insights into aspects of the South Asian worlds that I partially share with him and his gentle prodding in directions I had not considered have been invaluable. I hope he knows that he has my abiding gratitude. I began my early thinking about English and Vernacular education about 15 years ago with Professors C.K. Seshadri and Ranu Vanikar in Baroda, India and continued strains of it with Professors James Gee and Robert B. Kaplan in the USA. I began to take early steps toward conceptualizing my thoughts with Dwight Atkinson (in 1995) who continues to remain a source of stimulating and critical feedback. I also owe a great deal to Tommi Grover of Mulilingual Matters for believing in the value of the present project and to Nancy Hornberger and Colin Baker, the series editors, for including it in their series, and to Frances Fawkes for her careful and thorough reading of this typescript. This production of this manuscript has had its challenging moments and if it has made it to print, it is only because of their efforts. I am grateful to the following for permission to integrate parts of my previous publications. A version of Chapter 3 appeared in *The Canadian Modern Language Review* (2002, 59: 1) and is reprinted here by permission of University of Toronto Press Incorporated. Sections of Chapter 6 appeared in the *TESOL Quarterly* (1999, Vol. 33, 2) and is reprinted here by permission. Some pages of Chapter 6 first appeared in *The Journal of Second Language*

Writing (2003, 12(2): 130–132, 145–147) and are reprinted here by permission from Elsevier.

My greatest debt I owe to my family – my husband, Jody, and daughter, Aasha – for not only providing the lighter moments during the entire process but for serving as sounding boards for my ideas and observations. My parents, to whom this book is dedicated, represent to me the intermingling of English and the Vernaculars, as nothing else can. Direct products of colonial times while rooted in home-grown Vernacular traditions, they at once let me see how relations between English and Vernaculars in postcolonial contexts are simultaneously overlapping and dichotomous, divisive and not. They live out the dominant metaphor of gulfs and bridges used in this book by showing me, often in unspoken, quiet ways, that if all gulfs need bridges, then the first step is to look for and understand gulfs. Bridges (and resistance), then, are not far behind, if not already there. This book remains a tribute to them.

Vai Ramanathan, Davis, CA
22 November 2003

Chapter 1

Introduction: Situating the Vernacular in a Divisive Postcolonial Landscape

The stronger sense of 'postcolonial' emerges when we consider this seeming paradox: that it takes anticolonial struggles to produce neocolonial conditions. The postcolonial condition is the perspective one enters when one has resolved that paradox, relished that irony of history, and moved on. Postcoloniality in this sense is not confined to any particular kind of geopolitical space: it applies equally to the experience of diasporic and autochthonous communities, settler colonies no less than to territories of indirect rule, South African apartheid no less than to Indian democracy. Resisting any simple periodising correlations, the postcolonial condition is not one of power secured and centrally exercised in certain times and places. It is rather a dispersal, a moving field of possibilities which everywhere carry within them the mutually entailing, intimately cohabiting negative and positive charges of both power and resistance.
(Pechey, 1994: 153)

But the problem of voice is a problem of multiplicity as well as a problem of representation. How many voices are concealed beneath the generalizations of reported speech in much ethnography? And how many voices clamor beneath the enquiries and interests of the single ethnographer? How can we construct our voices so that they can represent the diversity of voices we hear in the field? How can we construct…a dialogue that captures the encounter of our own many voices with the voices we hear and purport to represent? The problem of voice ('speaking for' and 'speaking to') intersects with the problem of place (speaking 'from' and speaking 'of'). (Appadurai, 1988: 17)

The landscape of the postcolonial encounter is dotted with revisionist histories that attempt to go 'beyond the mystifying amnesia of the colonial aftermath' (Gandhi, 1998: 16) and this book is an effort in this direction. In general, the task of postcolonial studies has been to revisit, remember and question the colonial past, while simultaneously acknowledging the complex reciprocal relationship of antagonism and desire between the colonizer and colonized. While several instruments of power were used in the colonizing process, several have stayed in the postcolonial aftermath, including the crucial instrument of language (Dua, 1994, 2001; Rajagopalan, 1999). Because postcolonial contexts harken back to colonial pasts (that relatively frozen stance of always looking over one's shoulder as one proceeds ahead), the idea of how much of the colonial is embedded in the postcolonial voice is fraught with tension and complexities. Where does one end and the other begin? At what point is the postcolonial voice a voice with its own legitimacy? Built into this murky notion of 'voice' are various shades of power and resistance, which together form a nexus that is constantly at play in postcolonial worlds, with particular contexts making this notion more palpable than the others. While this prism-like nexus – of voice, power and resistance – gets enacted in various forms in different contexts, the components of the nexus remain the same.

One realm where this nexus is apparent is in the domain of education and it is the ways in which this nexus gets played out in different schooling contexts that informs the heart of this book. Located specifically in the area of English and Vernacular language teaching and learning, the book offers a relatively multifaceted sketch of the dynamics between English and the Vernaculars and the ways in which these dynamics are complexly embedded in a range of macro-structures in India, and the forms this nexus takes in the larger language teaching enterprise. While the book does not, by any means, discount the role of the British Raj in the creation of the English–Vernacular divide (Guha, 1997; Naregal, 2001; Pennycook, 1998), it does seek to go beyond the Raj to address some current language-related issues. Several researchers (cf. Phillipson, 1992; Skutnabb-Kangas & Phillipson, 1995) have called attention to the ways in which the global spread of English threatens local, Vernacular languages and the power differential built into English and regional languages in multilingual cultures. Certainly, much of what is presented in this book can be interpreted in this light. Powerful macro-structures – including institutional policies, larger state and nation-wide policies and pedagogical materials – do align with each other to shape, produce and perpetuate power/knowledge inequalities between those who have access to English and those who do not. (Indeed, researchers such as Bruthiaux [2002] argue that enhancing Vernacular education is a crucial step toward improving basic living standards in the developing world.) However, because realities on the postcolonial ground are more complex, it is equally important to understand how the English–Vernacular divide is resisted, specifically mitigated and bridged (Canagarajah, 1999). 'English and Vernacular knowledge' –

their teaching and learning, and their general production and consumption – then, from this integrated perspective, needs to be understood as an embedded, multi-pronged enterprise whose general functioning include both a complex domination and an equally complex resistance. An intent throughout this interpretive project, then, is one that attempts to understand some local complexities involved in the general (tertiary-level) English–Vernacular enterprise with a view to discerning how students, teachers and institutions are located vis-à-vis each other in this larger endeavor. By closely documenting where and how college-going students get situated in the English–Vernacular canvas, the ways in which tertiary-level English disadvantages students educated in the Vernacular and the ways in which teachers and institutions work at integrating English and the Vernaculars, I am arguing that any understanding of English and Vernacular education has to begin first by locating them side by side (as opposed to arranging them in a hierarchy). Doing so is the first step not only in addressing language-related inequalities on the postcolonial ground but in recognizing ways in which English and the Vernaculars while simultaneously divided and dichotomous from some points of view are also simultaneously overlapping and conjoined.

Setting the Stage

The area of postcolonial studies in the last decade seems to have burgeoned into a sub-discipline of its own, so much so that there appears to be little consensus regarding its scope and content. Some of the dissension seems to spill over into the realm of whether to hyphenate the term or not, with some critics believing that 'post-colonialism' with a hyphen indicates a clear temporal marker in history (signifying the end of colonial rule). Others believe that the 'postcolonial condition is inaugurated with the onset rather than the end of colonial occupation' (Gandhi, 1998: 3) and, thus, they maintain that the unbroken term postcolonialism comes closer to capturing a fuller range of colonial consequences.

Whatever the nuances of the controversy, the various viewpoints in postcolonial studies can be seen, I believe, to wrestle with issues of 'voice', including finding voices by which to speak back to colonial powers. (It is indeed no small irony that postcolonialists often have to speak back in the colonizer's tongue!) In their Introduction to the collection of essays, *Past The Last Post: Theorizing Post-colonialism and Post-modernism*, Ian Adam and Helen Tiffin (1991: vii) maintain that postcolonialism can be said to have two archives, one which constructs it as 'writing…grounded in those societies whose subjectivity has been constituted in part by the subordinating power of European colonialism' and a second in which the postcolonial is conceived as a set of discursive practices involving 'resistance to colonialism, colonist ideologies, and their contemporary forms and subjectificatory legacies'. Highlighted in the first archive is a degree of subordination; highlighted in the second is a degree of resistance. While this bifurcation may be a useful starting point, it is crucial to recognize that there not only exists a whole range between subordination and resistance but that facets of subordination and resistance typically operate as two sides of the same coin, intertwined and wrapped as each is in the other. There are clearly isolatable facets in the socio-educational system of any culture – including the Indian educational landscape discussed in this book – that not only serve to highlight instances where each of these notions is at play but also arenas where prying them apart is not so easy. This complex contact zone – between colonialist and postcolonialist ideologies, domination and opposition, English-medium (EM) and Vernacular-medium (VM) – is where this book situates itself.[1] From particular vantage points, this book highlights the English–Vernacular chasm by focusing on particular social stratifications on the ground – class, gender, caste – where individual efforts are not necessarily foregrounded. But from other vantage points, the book is also oriented toward capturing local *resistances* by calling attention to how particular teachers and institutions engage in critical practice by negotiating with the larger labyrinth to mitigate English's divisive role and to bridge the English–Vernacular gulf proactively. The book, then, in an attempt to be comprehensive strives to straddle both gulfs and bridges: by highlighting the gulf, we are able to see how English and its accompanying *assumptions nexus* (discussed in Chapter 2) sustain and deepen the English–Vernacular divide. Likewise foregrounding critical practice allows us to see how chasms are bridged and integration sought.

As mentioned in the Preface, the discursive act of writing about both social stratifications and transformations – where they each seem to be divided into different sections of a chapter – belies the fluidity and overlapping nature of dominations and resistances. Because both are part of each other, writing about them in separate sections – as I have been forced to do for clarity's sake – runs the risk of overlooking the conjoined nature between the two. In real life, dominations and resistance exist together, simultaneously informing each other, whether in classrooms, hallways, canteens or parking lots. As we will see in the following chapters, several parts of the socio-educational landscape place EM and VM students in oppositional relationships; several other parts provide room for active defiance including outright opposition to English, proactive gestures promoting the Vernacular, as well as attempts at integrating English Language Teaching and Learning (ELTL) with local Vernaculars.

Throughout, the book attempts to underscore the idea that the English–Vernacular enterprise is a process that is contested (Bhattacharya, 1998). While there are traditions and 'discourses' (Gee, 1990) associated with each, and while we need to (for clarity's sake) address these separately – as this book will occasionally do – English and the Vernaculars in multilingual, postcolonial contexts such as India are completely intertwined.

'Voicing', English and ELTL in India

As will become evident, I will frequently use the term '(de) voicing' to refer to ways in which Vernacular languages are relegated to subordinate positions and to ways in which English is seen to open social doors. While this section does not, by any means, attempt to trace the history of the term 'voice', I briefly address some general ways and contexts in which it has recently been used.

One area where this term has a home has been in the realms of first- and second-language writing. Recent debates on 'voice' have raised concerns regarding how locally embedded the notion is, with several facets of the term being highlighted in different ways: in terms of cross-cultural problems in the English as a Second Language (ESL) writing classroom (Ramanathan & Atkinson, 1999; Ramanathan, 2002a), its counterpart in other cultures (Matsuda 2001), its relation to the identities of graduate-level students (Hirvela & Belcher, 2001) and its inherently personal and social nature (Prior, 2001). These papers, among others, wrestle with voice in the context of second language (L2) writing. Borrowing the notion from this realm, this book highlights the more political nuances of the term by attempting to understand it in postcolonial contexts: *being empowered to speak/read/write*, in other words, being 'en-voiced'. Drawing primarily from my current, long-term project regarding English in India, details of which follow, I will argue that concerns regarding postcolonial voice(s) have necessarily to consider the following questions: Who is given the opportunity to speak and how? Who is simultaneously rendered 'voice-less'? Who assumes the power to speak back? What (divisive) role does English literacy – writing/reading/speaking – play in this general (dis)empowering process? Chimerical and multifaceted, if voice is indeed a locally embedded and relative term, as previous research has pointed out, then relevant questions that need to be asked – at least in postcolonial contexts where English is often the language of power – have necessarily to begin with those listed here.

From certain angles, one could argue that 'voicing' in India seems to be distinctly related to the medium of instruction in which students are educated, with the system privileging one set of students over others. All

K–12 (kindergarten to 12th grade) students in India have the option of being educated in either one of India's 15 nationally recognized languages or in English (Gupta *et al.,* 1995; Pattanayak, 1981).[2] Those students opting to be educated in the Vernacular are introduced to English from the fifth grade on (in Gujarat), just as EM students are introduced to the Vernacular at the same grade level. While theoretically this makes for a relatively egalitarian approach at the K–12 scene – where a lot of children have the option of being educated in their mother tongues or a closely allied language and learning a foreign language – the picture at college level, as the ensuing chapters detail, becomes much murkier.[3] All 'prestigious', science-based disciplines at the tertiary level such as computer science, engineering, the hard sciences, pharmacy and medicine seem to be available only in English. This means that if the English proficiency of students educated in the Vernacular is deemed insufficient at the end of the 12th grade, which by and large is the case, they are denied access to these 'prestigious' disciplines. Furthermore, in instances when VM students are admitted to EM colleges, they face the uphill task of not only taking classes with their EM counterparts but of having to take the same set of state-mandated examinations in English. In many cases, this proves to be insurmountable for many low-income VM students[4] and many of them drop out of the educational system during and after college. Students schooled in the EM, in contrast, do not face this language barrier at the college level: not only do they have a relatively easier time accessing the various 'prestigious' disciplines, they also have a comparatively easier time getting through the required examinations. As we will see in the following chapters, it is no accident that the differences between EM and VM students seem to fall along class lines.

The accessibility that the Indian middle class has to English literacy is integrally tied to (what I call) the *'assumptions nexus'* (Chapter 2), a collective syndrome of values, aspirations, perspectives, motivations, behaviors and world views that the middle class has by the sheer virtue of just being so, a nexus that seems to remain out of reach for low-income VM students (Singh, 1998). Nation- and state-wide educational policies, institutional practices, curricular and pedagogical materials among other factors are aligned in specific ways so as simultaneously to engage in combined relations of power to empower the upper and middle classes in particular social ways that directly yield certain social goods. Engaging in an exercise wherein we try to disassemble the various and connected parts of this socio-educational system helps our understanding of English and Vernacular knowledge production and consumption.

An opposition-oriented perspective regarding these issues implies, among other things, searching for, identifying and studying where and how pockets of struggle, negotiation and critical practice situate themselves in this complex alignment of forces. Arriving at a relatively global picture of the system's general alignment allows us to begin to value and understand the forces attempting to counter the alignment and ways in which the Vernacular is valued and validated (as opposed to being devalued and erased). As we will see, opting to be schooled in the Vernacular can itself be seen as an act of resistance toward English. Toward showing how complexly resistance functions in this context, I will also address facets of opposition including ways in which teachers and particular institutions work with state- and nation-wide policies to ensure that VM students get the extra help they need and the ways in which VM students negotiate how much importance to accord English in their daily lives without losing sight of their Vernacular roots. My aim, thus, will be two-fold: (1) to delineate different ways in which knowledge is organized, channeled and regulated; and (2) to ground the different types of organized knowledge and resistance in local contexts. My thesis is that what is regarded as 'knowledge' in any society/culture is fully realized within highly institutionalized (formal) social contexts (Tsoukas, 1998) and is shaped by the social practices emanating from and (re)produced by a range of central and peripheral contexts (Candlin & Mercer, 2001). Toward this end, the book attempts to understand a range of issues impacting on English and Vernacular literacy events both in the formal and non-formal arena, including those that may not be initially directly tied to our commonplace understanding of literacy. As Street (2002: 11) maintains, it is imperative that we 'start talking to people, listening to them, and linking their immediate experience out to other things that they do as well'. Attempting to understand how students, teachers and institutions wrestle with the English–Vernacular system as they are positioned in it and how facets of the system impact their overall knowledge production and consumption in a range of school and out-of-school realms will be the book's focus.

Before I proceed with the details of the book, I should reiterate a note that I mention in the Preface. The English I am talking about in this book is Indian English, a variety that is a splintered one, nativized as it has become over the last 300 years. VM and EM students in India can be seen to be placed on divergent points of the biliteracy continua (Hornberger, 2000), with degrees of nativization being more heightened in some school-related settings than others.

Details about the Book

This book is not intended to be read as a fully fledged 'ethnography' or as a 'critical study', although it undoubtedly has features of both (a critical ethnography' perhaps?). The 'researching' endeavor for this project – as with all long-term, extended studies – is far too complex and fluid to be neatly slotted into particular research types/categories. Indeed, I am using the terms 'research', 'researching', 'study' in quotes because I wish to call attention to their generally problematic nature. The reasoning behind this emphasis stems partly from a growing understanding that the researcher always has an impact on the 'researching' scene, that there is no 'objective' distanced observer and that as 'researchers' we are a part of those we 'study'. Endeavors such as this one are not 'studies' as much as they are extensions of our understanding of the worlds we seek to better comprehend. Indeed, this current general exercise of 'writing-up' my understanding of some realities on the ground is a most artificial break in what I see as a continuing and evolving understanding of the complexities of some divergent educational scenes.

The local realities presented here are based in the city of Ahmedabad in Gujarat, India (I address my own biases as researcher presently). A native of the city and as one who spent the first 23 years of my life there, I have witnessed firsthand the kinds of problems that several of my VM friends (Gujarati, in the present case) encountered with English at the tertiary level. Some were constantly on the verge of dropping out because they found English classes too difficult. Many felt enormous pressure to perform in examinations and would even go to great lengths to get 'leaked' examination questions prior to the examination date in order to prepare responses to them. Only much later in my graduate education and teaching career and during the 'research' for this project did I realize how their problems were integrally tied to local institutional, state- and nation-wide educational policies and practices. Although I had done my K–12 and BA in Ahmedabad's institutions and was thus familiar with the general workings of the system when I began this research, some state-wide and institutional polices regarding ELTL had changed. Thus, as a 'researcher', I returned to some of these sites as an outsider (having lived outside the culture for the previous 14 years) and as a relative former insider (having been raised and schooled in India and having attended one of the institutions explored here). The combination of being and feeling both an insider and outsider to the institutional scenes has been, for the most part, an asset: I was able to gain access to materials and information that a 'non-*Ahmedabadi*' (someone not native to Ahmedabad) may not have had, I was also able to see and react to scenes with a defamiliarized, 'sociological attitude' that permits 'the sociologist to observe the conduct of self and others' (Vidich & Lyman, 1994: 23). Throughout the exploring process, I was very conscious of seeming a neocolonialist, representing to VM teachers some of the very qualities they are resisting in their work toward enhancing the Vernaculars. This awareness – that I was very much in the category of 'you EM people' (*tum English-medium vaalo*) for these teachers – enabled me to approach my group discussions with VM teachers with a strong intent to understand and learn from their points of view. This combination of being a relative 'outsider' and 'insider' is partially captured in the unevenness in the 'voices' I adopt in the various chapters. (In Chapters 2 and 3, for instance, I attempt to step back from the scene, while in Chapters 4, 5 and 6, I am more present. I address this variation of my insertions into my writing in the respective chapters.)

Throughout this interpretive endeavor – including the 'data-gathering' process and the writing of it – I adopt what Greene and Bloome (1997: 183) call an *ethnographic perspective*, whereby I take a 'focused approach to study particular aspects of everyday [school] life and cultural practices of a social group', with theories of culture and inquiry practices from anthropology or sociology permeating all aspects of the researching endeavor. The writing process, as with many long-term qualitative projects, has been and continues to be a messy one (Atkinson, 1992; Clifford, 1990; Sanjek, 1990), vacillating constantly between the three activities that inform the naturalistically oriented enterprise: inscription, transcription and description (Clifford, 1990). While these are completely artificial terms, since researching and writing processes 'blend or alternate rapidly in the shifting series of encounters' (Clifford, 1990: 52), I found that occasionally and consciously breaking up the researching process into these steps served the valuable function of defamiliarizing a (too) familiar scene. Moving constantly between the acts of making 'mental notes' (inscription), writing them down at the first opportunity (transcription) and reflecting on and making sense of them (description) – and not necessarily in the linear order implied here – was a crucial part of the researching process. The fact that the understanding and exploration of each segment of the long-term project built successively on previous ones – where unanswered questions from an earlier leg of the project were carried over to understanding the next – contributed to the overall depth of my general understanding of the issues involved. It allowed me to see, for example, how different institutions wrestled with language policy issues to address a core set of English and Vernacular issues in that context.

One of the bigger cities in the state (the state has an estimated population of 40 million), Ahmedabad is primarily a commercial hub, with a lot of its citizens engaged in businesses of various sorts. It has, over the last decade, given the liberalizing of the country's economy, seen a growing surge in its middle-class population. While the city, like most Indian cities, has speakers of several different languages, it officially recognizes Gujarati,

Hindi and English. Most Ahmedabadis are able to converse in at least two out of the three.

Three divergent institutional realities inform this project: the first is a middle-class largely EM Jesuit institution that has recently opened its doors to those VM students that are simultaneously low caste and low-income;[5] the second is a low-income VM women's college; and the third is an EM private business college that admits a few VM students (depending on their English proficiency). Access to these sites happened gradually and in a chain-like fashion. Because I had done my BA at the Jesuit college, I was familiar with the management and they gave me permission to conduct my research. One of the faculty members at this college happened to know the chair of the English Department at the women's college and I was able, through him, to get permission from the principal and teachers to conduct some of my research there. At this institution, one of the faculty members mentioned a teacher who used to work with them but now taught at the business college. I was able to track this person down (who, it turned out, had done his BA at the Jesuit college) and through him get in touch with the management and faculty at this institution. The issue of Vernaculars and VM students seemed to touch a sensitive chord in all three institutions, with most people indicating a strong willingness not just to help me with my research but to share their opinions and point to complexities that I may not have thought of. Together, all three institutions highlight interesting facets of the Ahmedabad educational scene. The women's college and the private business institution represent two ends of a class spectrum, with each contending with Vernacular–English issues very differently. While the English–Vernacular chasm informs the Jesuit college as well, this institution represents particular pro-Vernacular orientations in its overall activist stance. Thus, while all three colleges wrestle with some common issues – including particular state- and nation-wide policies – each institution opens up particular ways in which the Vernacular is both valued and validated, as well as de-valued and threatened.

At the risk of making this sound like a 'positivistic' 'study' (when it is not) that can get tidily 'written up' in neat sections of a typical 'research' project, I would like to explain the nature and extent of my 'data'. I am most self-conscious and, to some extent, anxious as to how I am framing the exploration offered here: as mentioned earlier, I am writing about people in my home city and thus, in a sense, am one of them; however, I am also writing about peoples whose life experiences have been different from mine which I am trying, quite systematically, to understand. This dynamic of being simultaneously an 'insider' and 'outsider' is a fraught, tension-filled position and the current act of writing about it not only fails to capture my ambiguities about my role and conflicts but also imposes a simplistic veneer on that landscape and this writing that, from some angles, is quite plainly incomplete (I address my biases and motivations regarding this exploration presently). The raw materials on which this project is based consists of a range of 'data types' including interviews with over 80 Gujarati and EM students, 21 faculty members, over 100 hours of classroom observations and extensive written documents (including university-mandated syllabi, sample examination questions, student responses, textbooks, notices and circulars and advertisements of various programmes, and newspaper articles and opinion pieces on educational issues). Most of these materials were gathered primarily during the summer months in the last seven years. Some written documents – such as student evaluations and teaching reflections – were gathered through the regular academic years. (Particulars regarding materials from each of the institutions are addressed in the relevant chapters.)

While this wealth of material represents a range of obvious and latent issues, the book isolates three strands for detailed investigation. These strands are: (1) divergent pedagogic tools, (2) divergent pedagogic practices and (3) divergent tracks. I justify this selectiveness in this way: (1) all three strands are superordinate social cogs with diverse sub-cogs that can be seen to maintain the EM–VM gulf; (2) all three strands have interesting historical trajectories that extend from India's colonial past and find distinct articulation in the present; and (3) all three cumulatively inform the overall context against which to understand local resistances. While the book does not, by any means, aim to offer a comprehensive review of all the social sub-cogs or extensive historical accounts of current postcolonial structures, it does point out how the intertwined nature of the social cogs informs current realities on the ground. By no means linear or simple – as may be implied in the way in which I have broken them down here and elsewhere in the book – the social cogs are *aligned* (Wartenberg, 1990) with each other to produce an elaborate socio-educational machinery that through English knowledge – and its general production and consumption – simultaneously sustains the English–Vernacular gulf while seeming to envoice the EM over their VM counterparts. My presenting these strands as disparate and separable, then, while running the risk of being reductive, is done primarily to highlight how and where VM students are positioned in the larger landscape. Although I have attempted as much as possible to situate each strand within particular institutional contexts to highlight how they each operate locally, all three strands inform each other simultaneously and work as interlocking pieces that hold the larger socio-educational apparatus together.

Strand 1: The Politics of Divergent Pedagogic Tools

Toward setting the stage for understanding why VM students struggle the way they do at college level, the book will offer a close analysis of the divergent cultural models regarding English literacy that VM and EM students are socialized into at the K–12 levels, with the latter winning out over the former. While the term 'cultural models' is hard to pin down, it shapes human behavior in obvious and latent ways and informs our respective 'takes'/slants/orientations on all the things in the world. Scholars such as Shore believe that 'cultural models' refer to 'an extensive and heterogenous collection of "models" that exist both as public artifacts "in the world" and as cognitive constructs "in the minds" of members of a community' (Shore, 1996: 44) and one arena in which divergent cultural models seem obvious is in the different English language textbooks used in VM and EM K–12 settings.

Because textbooks serve as key instruments through which knowledge is transmitted and consumed, thus functioning as valuable tools in the schooling domain, examining them closely not only allows us to see how they connect with divergent teaching practices but also affords some understanding of why VM students using these texts find themselves, by and large, either shut out of EM colleges or struggling very hard to cope. As we will see, these textbooks seem to contribute to producing two very different 'literate-in-English' candidates. The combination of particular kinds of metadiscourse, the westernized readings, the relative space for individual views and opinions, the comprehension exercises that ask students to probe and reason about civic and social issues in the EM texts are partially based on a set of teaching and learning practices that prepare one kind of 'literate-in-English' person. In contrast, the combination of alternative metadiscourses, an extensive focus on grammar and survival English, and the general lack of space for self-learning and essay writing in VM textbooks shape very different 'literate-in-English' candidates.

It is this set of divergent cultural models that VM and EM students bring with them to the college scene, a divergence that has serious consequences for VM students. Some teachers at the college level – both VM and EM – recognize the importance of altering and negotiating with pedagogic practices as ways of getting students to prepare for graduate school and to look beyond immediate exit examinations. For some teachers, efforts at resisting the machinery and engaging in meaningful critical practices emerge in a range of local ways: including supplementing textbooks with extra readings (that are not part of the examination syllabus), to holding day-long, intensive seminars on particular interdisciplinary topics, to challenging the ways in which students think about looking beyond examinations. This is not to say that these teachers are not frustrated by the constraints of the larger educational enterprise – as one of them puts it, he has had to learn ways of 'trying to beat the system on the job' – but that the oppositional endeavor is evident and in some cases prominently so. Students too recognize the extra efforts some teachers make to go beyond the mandated syllabus, efforts that are particularly meaningful and poignant to low-income VM students.

Strand 2: The Politics Related to Divergent Pedagogic Practices

The book will also explore some ways in which pedagogic practices differ according to mediums of instruction at the college level and the need to understand these differences in terms of issues 'peripheral' to the classroom, including those related to nation- and state-wide language policies and the socio-cultural worlds of EM and VM students. While it is certainly the case that the 'classroom doesn't have to be at the mercy of power dictated unilaterally from above', as will be evident in the resistance efforts of teachers (Canagarajah, 1999b: 11), the book will also point out that classrooms are not entirely autonomous domains, free of macro-structures and that much of the divergence in pedagogic practices that teachers use can be seen to be allied with class-related attitudes and practices that fall along the lines of mediums of instruction. Such an interconnected understanding is crucial since without understanding the relationships for [lack of] support for 'English or Vernacular languages and other material and discursive forces of colonialism, we will have an inadequate appreciation of both colonialism and current [postcolonial] language policies' (Pennycook, 1998: 69).

Toward highlighting the differences between pedagogic practices, the book offers an in-depth examination of two divergent institutions – one a low-income, VM women's college and the other an upper middle-class, EM business college – with a view to exploring how the different socio-educational practices operate in each. Socio-educational practices, as the book will attempt to exemplify, is a confluence of a range of factors including Vernacular traditions, pedagogical tools, learning styles, teaching practices, latent historical and current ideological forces and state- and nation-wide language policies, with clusters of some of these factors more dominant in some contexts than in others. As we will see, patterns of these clusters can fall along the lines of mediums of instruction. A relatively multidimensional understanding of the inter-relations of several of these features affords insight into how English *versus* Vernacular knowledge production and consumption remain, from some points of view, as distinct enterprises, while also revealing areas of overlap, where some teachers freely draw on

Vernacular traditions, myths and ways of learning and teaching toward enhancing student development. While the juxtaposition of the two contrasting worlds is deliberate – since I wish to call attention to the divisive role that English plays – the efforts by teachers to reach out to VM students (in both settings) by finding ways of connecting their teaching to their students' Vernacular backgrounds point to ways in which teachers actively, in small ways, go about resisting the inequalities built into the larger system. Ranging from how teachers intervene to negotiate with parents regarding keeping students in college, to how students find ways of dealing with examinations and unfair assessment, to how institutions interpret state-level educational policies to open their doors to the underprivileged, the book will also document the ways in which dominant alignments (Ramanathan, 2002a; Wartenberg, 1990) and general 'devoicing' are countered.

Strand 3: The Politics of Tracking and the General Preference for Teaching English Literature

Combined with the two previous strands is the third skein of tracking students into separate 'streams': those who are allowed to major in English (primarily literature) and those who are not. While both tracking and literature teaching are, to a large extent, a result of state-mandated education policies, the local ways in which they are worked out in particular institutions vary. Situating these points in the context of a Jesuit institution committed to improving the lives of those VM students who are also of 'low-caste' and low-income backgrounds, the book will uncover ways in which the institution negotiates with and around state-mandated policies of tracking and literature-teaching while staying committed to its ideals. Assuming a position of critical opposition in its assertion of empowering low-caste, VM students, the institution struggles with problems facing other institutions in the state: faculty who are trained as literature instead of language teachers, the adoption of teaching methods that do not particularly enhance the communicative abilities of VM students and a relatively large gulf between what (VM) students wish they could get out of their English classes and current state-mandated syllabi. Despite these inhibiting macro-structures, however, the institution finds local ways to circumnavigate the more 'oppressive' aspects of state- and nation-wide policies: opening its doors specifically to low-caste students, helping particular groups of VM students with extra English classes, finding ways to mitigate the gulf between EM and VM students in extra-curricular activities in the college. As with the earlier themes, this one too will aim at revealing some of the disempowering facets that VM students have to contend with while being mindful of how institutions work to bridge the English–Vernacular gulf.

As mentioned earlier, these strands constitute major cogs in the English–Vernacular enterprise at the tertiary level in India and viewing them as overlapping and intersecting components, despite my isolating and itemizing them, is crucial. My use of the term 'voicing' begs uncovering as well. My unravelling of some of the complex ways in which VM students are positioned in the larger system is intended to clarify the divisive role that English plays: how various aspects of the socio-educational apparatus seem to work synchronously to empower (and thus 'en-voice') the EM counterparts while simultaneously shutting doors on VM students. My efforts at searching for, documenting and understanding how the status quo is questioned and resisted by students and teachers is not only intended to recognize how individuals are placed in this system but to underscore the idea that all (systemic) dominations have critical forces countering them, and that researchers engaged in understanding the larger social picture need to address local elements of both.

Complex and thorny as matters of research orientations are, they point directly to the researchers' theoretical and political biases and it is important that I lay these bare, since they touch on the crucial realm of the politics of representation. As I mention in the Preface, it is because I am a 'native' to the culture – indeed the city of Ahmedabad, although I am not Gujarati – that I feel compelled to call attention to educational practices and structures that seem to deny entire groups of students equal access to the society's social goods. As a researcher who is interested in addressing language-related inequalities in educational realms, demystifying some of the ways in which power emanates from and flows through particular macro-structures in the Gujarat context becomes a way by which to understand how and why VM students remain in their disadvantaged positions. If I addressed only the active pockets of opposition, when I know – having been bred by the system and having spent several years attempting to understand the English–Vernacular gulf – I run the risk of not providing the full picture (and thus, by extension, of seeming 'dishonest'). As much as possible, I have tried to call attention to both gulfs and bridges around English and the Vernaculars.

Questions and issues of what are 'present' and 'absent' clearly underlie what are 'visible' and 'invisible' in literacy events and practices and are determined, to a large extent, by the researcher's lens. What I have selected to include and leave out are, therefore, a result of deliberate choices I have made. What is included in this landscape, how it has been *languaged* into existence and the connections I have made between practices, events, polices, institutions, and choices are thus, crucially tied to my role in this exploratory endeavor. As an upper-caste, middle-class, Indian female, in her late thirties, educated in the EM, I undoubtedly influenced the very scenes I was attempting to understand. Indeed, my class and caste status undoubtedly influence what students or teachers do/do not share with me (especially in Chapters 4 and 5). What is presented here, then, is the sense I have made (and this continues to evolve) of the current English–Vernacular divide. Hyperconscious as I have now become of being 'one of the EM [neo-colonial] types', I am also consciously seeking to create a textual space in research, whereby resistance to English is acknowledged, understood and addressed. This act of writing about postcolonialism – when I am a post-colonial product myself – is rife with contradictions. Most notable among the contradictions is that while I am seemingly *anti*colonial in my privi-leging the Vernacular, I am simultaneously neocolonial in my writing of Vernacular issues. By writing about issues important to VM students and teachers, I could, in fact, be seen as 'constructing' them and speaking for them. The only justification I have for doing so is that Vernacular-related issues in India or the larger subcontinent at large have received very little attention and almost all the VM students and teachers to whom I have spoken want these issues to be fore-fronted. My entire discussion here, then, treads on unstable ground: I am attempting to understand some pro-Vernacular sentiments when I am seen as a product of the very ideologies they are trying to resist. My discussion, thus, is to be understood as being situated in a contact zone 'within an area of tension between definition and powerlessness to define, between containment of my subject and recogni-tion of its uncontained plurality' (Spurr, 1993: 2).

I hope that my general focus on the ways in which some of the aligned social structures stack up against VM students is not read to mean that I am promoting ELTL as 'the answer' for this group of students. Indeed, nothing could be further from the truth. My intention is to get a better grasp of the complexities on the postcolonial ground; i.e. to see where English can be seen to play a divisive role, and where Vernaculars compete with English and are validated from other angles. These are realities that all of us TESOLers/Applied Linguists need to be aware . Understanding how local conditions work toward constituting language-related social practices will better enable us to understand the murky waters that VM students and teachers have to traverse in their learning and teaching processes. As we will see, socio-educational practices are a complex syndrome of several interlocking factors and while I have, for the purposes of analysis, held up some clusters of these forces for closer inspection in the different chapters, I have tried, on the whole, to integrate and reconnect these clusters to the larger system of which they are a part. Also part of the larger enterprise is the 'writing up' on my part: this writing process – much as I am resisting it – imposes a linear, logical, sequential quality to what are very diverse, dichotomous, disparate realities. The unevenness between my roles as 'native' and 'researcher', 'insider' and 'outsider' along with the voices of teachers, students and administrators competitively insist themselves on all dimensions of my writing: interpreting, explaining, understanding and formulating. Indeed, as will be evident, in some of the chapters I partially highlight my role as 'outsider' by not inserting myself into the writing; in other chapters I make room for my positioning and participation. If the presentation of these divergent realities emerges as smooth and coherent, it is a smoothness and coherence that has been imposed and manufactured from my pen: if there is an unevenness, it is because of my uncertainty and ambiguity regarding my positioning in this overall endeavor. As mentioned earlier, by breaking the complexities on the ground into chasms and bridges, I belie the intertwined and contradictory nature of dominations and countering forces. This split is a construction entirely of my making. As 'researcher' and 'native', I am fully and completely embedded in and producer of this construction.

Connections to Applied Linguistics/TESOL

This type of embedded, local understanding of how English is mired in the macro- and micro-structures of a multilingual and postcolonial context such as India is important for at least two reasons. For one, it allows us to understand areas of friction and cooperation between the teaching and learning of different languages in the same/similar cultural domain. Exploring how ELTL is positioned vis-à-vis the teaching and learning of Vernaculars in the same context affords us glimpses into areas of overlap and divergences. Sanskrit, Gujarati, Hindi and English language teaching and learning are negotiated in very different ways at both classroom and institutional levels and understanding how students and teachers see them as separate yet similar endeavors reveals partial yet crucial insights about the culture's language teaching practices, attitudes and orientations in general. Being aware of how local constraints – including the teaching of parallel Vernacular languages – inform spontaneous decisions teachers and students make as they relate to each other and their curricular materials, as well as larger generalized views students and teachers evolve about 'successful' language learning and teaching will nuance ways in which we teacher-educators and researchers conceive of and present the larger ELTL enterprise.

Another way in which the book will contribute to current research in

Applied Linguistics and TESOL is in the area which is sometimes referred to as 'second first language'. While there is a sizeable amount of research on second-language development, exploring how entire groups of people in multilingual contexts have two first languages has not been adequately studied (Baker, 2000). Hornberger's (2000) comprehensive framework of the *continua of biliteracy* reminds us of the social, political and cultural implications of how speakers negotiate between two first languages, the ways in which learners are positioned on different points of several co-existing literacy continua, the pockets of competition they feel between the languages and the ways in which one language gets particular reinforcement and value over the other (in different contexts) sheds light on the complexity of this phenomenon. Indeed, many of the EM students in this exploration fall into this category and while the book will not offer an in-depth analysis of this particular issue, it will certainly, where relevant, call attention to the conflict EM students feel between their two first languages.

Chapter-wise Breakdown of the Book

Toward partially explicating the struggles of VM students at tertiary levels of education and toward providing a backdrop against which to understand some of the divergent knowledge-production scenes presented in the book, Chapter 2 will offer a synthesized account of several language-related social practices, including how several macro-structures align with each other to produce an elaborate social machinery that dovetails closely with the assumptions, values and orientations of the Indian middle class. Some of these macro-structures are related to English and Vernacular language policies, while others are concerned with enforced pedagogical and curricular practices. Also addressed will be the historical influence of particular figures such as Mahatma Gandhi and committees such as the 'Remove English Lobby' (REL) (*Angrezi Hatao Aandolan,*) whose collective views represent the conflict and chasm between English and the Vernaculars.

Toward a better understanding of the struggles of VM students at the college realm, Chapter 3 concentrates on a key facet of the K–12 educational scene, namely textbooks and the ways in which they are partially responsible for socializing two sets of students in markedly different ways. This chapter will argue that the divergence in the texts can be partially explained by the very different cultural models (regarding English literacy) that operate for the EM and VM respectively, a point that underscores the larger discussion of the English–Vernacular chasm. Moving away from this generalized state to addressing realities on the ground, Chapter 4 will be devoted to addressing how particular mediums of instruction entail complex, though divergent socio-cultural worlds within which English and the Vernaculars are placed. Contextualized in two vastly different institutions – one a VM, low-income women's college and the other an EM, co-educational private business college – the chapter calls attention to how pedagogic practices in classrooms reflect and are shaped by a range of issues in surrounding social worlds, including teachers' attitudes to their students, students' personal goals and the joint negotiations between teachers and students with curricular materials. These factors align themselves very differently in the two institutions with divergent consequences for the two sets of students, with one set of the students being consistently empowered in ways in which their counterparts are not. This chapter will also address ways in which teachers at both institutions find ways of countering the English–Vernacular gulf by engaging local forms of critical practice.

Moving toward examining two other key socio-educational cogs – namely tracking and a focus on literature – Chapter 4 will call attention to how these two state-mandated educational practices work together to maintain the English–Vernacular gulf and how one particular institution works to bridge the chasm despite these regulations. While focusing on reaching out to a particularly underprivileged section of VM students, this chapter will highlight issues related to tracking (and literature teaching) that plague other EM colleges in the city. The last chapter of the book (Chapter 6) will tease out key strands covered in the previous chapters while extending the debate to address some latent issues including how language policies become social practices, how the divisive and/or integrative relationship between the Vernaculars and English have to be understood in local terms, what this understanding means for the phrase 'global English(es)' and the near impossibility of separating colonial policy and postcolonial practice. It will address these issues toward partially answering the following questions: What do such findings mean for those of us in the larger language teaching enterprise? How do we best understand 'critical practices'? It will also underscore the need for all of us in applied linguistics and TESOL – to engage in repeatedly uncovering the purpose and politics of what we do or claim to do. English, as we shall see, through particular lenses and in some parts of the world, divides.

A glossary of abbreviations used

ELTL: English language teaching and learning
VM: Vernacular medium
EM: English medium
FI: Faculty interview
SI: tudent interview

Notes

1. I am using the terms EM and VM for pragmatic reasons. Hyphenated as these terms are, they tend to be discursively cumbersome. I am very aware of the fact that they could be regarded as 'labels' and wish to make my intentions in my usage of them clear. I should also point out that while VM can, for a lot of students and teachers, mean mother-tongue education, it is not necessarily always the case. There are at least a few (VM) students in this project that have Marathi at their mother tongue but who have opted to be educated in Gujarati because there is not a good enough Marathi-medium school in Gujarat and because their parents prefer education in any VM over an education in English.
2. These 15 languages – contained in the 'Eighth Schedule' of the constitution – are: Assamese, Bangla, Gujarati, Hindi, Kashmiri, Kannada, Marathi, Malayalam, Oriya, Punjabi, Tamil, Telegu, Urdru, Sanskrit and Sindhi. For studies on literacy practices in South Asia, see Brian Street's (2002) edited volume entitled *Literacy and Development: Ethnographic Perspectives* (London: Routledge).
3. For a critical and detailed discussion of the numerous minority languages left out of the eight schedule, see Gupta *et al.* (1995). Specifically, see the essays by Krishnamurti, Khubchandani, Pattanayak, Gargesh, Ahmad, Dua and Kullar.
4. Not all VM students come from low-income homes. There is a sizeable group of middle-class VM students in Ahmedabad. This group, however, is, relatively speaking, much smaller than those from low-income homes; also, middle-class VM students have access to English (private classes, tutorials) in ways that low-income VM students do not.
5. Class, caste and medium-of-instruction do not necessarily go hand-in-hand. This particular Jesuit institution has begun to welcome those low-caste students that are poor and have been schooled in the Vernacular. Other colleges in the state generally follow the statutory government quotas.

Chapter 2

Divisive Postcolonial Ideologies, Language Policies and Social Practices

The need for a 'sociology of knowledge' is thus already given with the observable differences between societies in terms of what is taken for granted as 'knowledge' in them...In other words, a 'sociology of knowledge' will have to deal not only with the empirical variety of 'knowledge' in human societies, but also with the processes by which any *body of 'knowledge' comes to be socially established as 'reality...'. It is our contention, then, that the sociology of knowledge must concern itself with whatever passes for 'knowledge' in a society, regardless of the ultimate validity or invalidity (by whatever criteria) of such 'knowledge'. And insofar as all human 'knowledge' is developed, transmitted and maintained in social situations, the sociology of knowledge must seek to understand the processes by which this is done in such a way that a taken-for-granted 'reality' congeals for the man in the street. In other words, we contend that the sociology of knowledge is concerned with the analysis of the social construction of reality.*

(Berger & Luckman, 1967: 3)

Berger and Luckman's quote succinctly captures one of the overall aims I have for this book: to uncover and understand how knowledge is produced and consumed and how the reproduction of and resistance to a complex set of social alignments together comprise an elaborate socio-educational landscape. The 'sociology of knowledge' orientation advocated in the quote (and partially explicated in this chapter and the rest of the book) provides a valuable conceptual background for understanding some of the social practices surrounding English and the Vernaculars in multilingual contexts. Ideologies and 'discourses' (Gee, 1990), as we know, shape most key sites in the educational arena, including institutional and classroom behaviors as well as pedagogical practices and tools which, with their constant re-enactment and practice over time, become 'commonsensical' and 'naturalized'. In an effort to understand and problematize several related constructs, including ideologies, historicizing, social practices and language policies, this chapter attempts to provide a partial overview of how they combine together to form and inform any socio-educational system.

This chapter is organized as follows. The first section will first offer a general discussion of ideologies and thought collectives (Ramanathan, 2002a) before moving on to addressing historicizing and colonizing as discursive practices. This section will also address ways in which socio-educational practices on the ground are embedded in ideologies. Toward explicating some of the abstract points in the first section, the second section will specifically attend to ways in which two particular anti-English and pro-Vernacular ideologies – Gandhi's pro-Vernacular sentiments and those of the Remove English Lobby (REL) – crucially inform and sustain the English–Vernacular gulf by becoming reified into particular national- and state-wide language policies. Moving specifically into the realm of class-related ideologies, the third section will explore ways in which the values and aspirations of the Indian middle class dovetail with this complex socio-educational system to form an *assumptions nexus*, a construct that partially explains how the overall apparatus works to maintain the status quo. It is against this elaborate network of practices that domains of negotiation, resistance and critical practice of students, teachers and institutions need to be understood. As will be evident in the following pages, the 'voice' I am deliberately adopting here is a relatively more 'distanced' one: not only am I am trying to arrive at a relatively interconnected sense of some historical and current realities that shape language learning and teaching by (artificially) attempting to stand back from what is my own home turf, I am also trying to bring together some conceptual ways of framing issues that emerge in the remainder of the book.

Ideologies and Thought Collectives: Knowledge Production and Consumption

It goes without saying that the socio-educational practices in any culture are a complex convergence of several intertwining factors and local realities on the ground are produced, shaped and sustained by particular ideological and historical forces. (Indeed, the effort to disentangle local realities from ideologies is futile, since we will never fully know which 'causes' which.) Ideologies, generated, sustained and reproduced by communities of practices, are parts of 'thought collectives' (see Ramanathan [2002a] for a detailed discussion of this term). Circulated over and between members of a collective, a shared thought structure, produced by structure, produced by 'common understanding and mutual misunderstanding' (Fleck, 1981), generates similar ways of being, thinking, behaving and believing, and includes, as in the present case, conceptualizing and the teaching and learning of Vernacular languages. This relative emphasis on a 'shared thought structure' is not to imply that pockets of difference and divergence do not exist; indeed, as I have explained at length elsewhere (Ramanathan, 2002a), institutions and individuals constantly pick and choose from the tenets of their thought collectives, ones they wish to enhance, change and reproduce, thus, over time, producing different thought collectives, sometimes in resistance to previously existing ones. (For a fuller discussion of ideologies, see Pannikar [1998] and Eagleton [1991].) Indeed, as we shall see in Chapter 5, the pedagogic choices that teachers make in particular settings echo strains of particular ideologies.

This discussion of thought collectives helps us partially to understand the impossibility of ever figuring out when an 'ideology' emerges as a form of 'resistance' to other overlapping thought structures and when the (once) resistance ideology assumes a life-force of its own (to the point where the original tenets it was resisting are sometimes hard to locate in the collective memory). The pro-Vernacular stances adopted by Gandhi during his struggle for Indian Independence and the anti-English stance implicit in the REL examined in this chapter can be seen, to some extent, to illustrate these points. Gandhi's call for freedom and national unity was indivisibly tied to his views on language: he consistently maintained that a new, liberated India could only fully emerge if it fully and completely enhanced the Vernaculars and gave up being enslaved by all things British, including, of course, the crucial instrument of colonization, namely the English language. The REL, which can be seen as a thought collective of its own (with formal documents in the 1970s), can, on the one hand, be seen to draw much of its energy and motivations from Gandhi's nationalistic pro-Vernacular stance. In other ways, it needs also to be acknowledged and addressed as a movement of its own, emerging almost 30–40 years after Gandhi and emphasizing as it did a kind of grassroots, local activism. As we will see, some of the VM teachers make explicit connections to Gandhi's ideologies; others articulate views that seem to resonate more strongly with the REL. Still others view 'English domination' as part of a larger surge toward general 'English madness' (*Angrezi Paagalpan*). For this last set of people – some of whom are staunchly Gandhian as well – the current craze for English – English programmes on TV, state-level policies to introduce English instruction at earlier grade levels in VM schools, westernized ways of dressing and using language – which they see in their children and students needs to be actively resisted. By saying that (EM and VM) teachers seem to draw on these linked-but-separate thought structures, I do not mean to make crude distinctions between their views and the thought collectives that spawn them; indeed, the very nature of thought collectives and their ideologies evades such fixing. What I am trying to underscore is the idea that teachers (especially of VM students) draw on different strains of thought when articulating their pro-Vernacular/anti-English sentiments (Chapters 5 and 6), sentiments that can sometimes be seen to echo more closely with one thought collective than the other. In this sense, the exercise of attempting to connect classroom practice with ideological currents is an interpretive one. A direct one-to-one mapping between ideological currents and actual practice is just as (im)possible as a direct mapping between thought and language: there is always an element of fuzziness built into the enterprise.

Ideologies and Historicizing In and Through Writing

Addressing current social realities – in any realm – in terms of selective aspects of the past runs the risk of imposing on past (and, to some extent, current) events a linearity and chronology that is more an entity in the author's/historian's head than it is a 'fact' or set of actualities. Chakrabarty (2000: 247) states that there at least two kinds of relationships to the past.

> One is historicism, the idea that to get a grip on things we need to know their histories, the process of development they have undergone in order to become what they are…The idea is that once one knows the causal structures that operate in history, one may also gain a certain mastery of them.

The other is what he calls 'decisionism', whereby the author/historian 'guided by his or her values to choose the most desirable, sane, and wise future for humanity…looks to the past as a warehouse of resources on which to draw as needed'. The discussion offered in this book definitely draws on both aspects of reconstructing the past: toward partially understanding why VM college teachers in Gujarat make the pedagogic choices they do, I occasionally attempt to 'reconstruct' aspects of the ideologies on which they draw (Chapters 5 and 6), since these ideologies are strongly associated with particular historical figures and movements. As mentioned in the Introduction, the current understanding of some language-related complexities in a postcolonial context is very slippery, caught as I am between postcolonialism and subjection, on the one hand, and neocolonialism and power, on the other.

Ideologies and Socio-educational Practices

Relevant to the previous points about ideologies is the idea of how institutions partially legitimize particular ideologies and the ways in which language policies and social practices, in both institutions and in class-rooms, reflect aspects of larger free-floating ideologies (Bauldauf & Luke, 1990; Hornberger, 1995; Ricento, 2000). An 'institution', according to Berger (1963), is a body that regulates distinctive and complex social actions, a definition general enough to permit a view of social structures as including class, law, marriage or (organized) religion as institutions. From such a point of view, an institution is a regulatory agency that channels human behavior and thought. Indeed, in the light of the present study, labels and terms associated with educational institutions ('pass/fail', 'appropriate/inappropriate', 'fluent/limited', 'advanced tracks', 'honors students') are partial ways by which human behavior is molded and regu-lated.

In other words, institutions provide procedures through which human [student] conduct is patterned, compelled to go, in grooves deemed desir-able by society. And this trick is performed by making these grooves appear to the individuals as the only possible ones. (Berger, 1963: 87)

As we will see in the ensuing chapters, particular institutional and statewide socio-educational practices – such as tracking students on the basis of their fluency in English, or setting up language-related gate-keeping criteria that make the 'prestigious' disciplines inaccessible to low-income VM students – drawn as they are from free-floating pro-Vernacular/anti-English sentiments, serve the function of grooves that can be seen to partially stratify both student and teacher behavior. Needless to say, such stratification seriously 'de-voices' VM students.

This issue of legitimization brings us to the discussion of social practices in general. What are social practices and how to do they work themselves out in the educational realm? What is their relation to ideologies and thought structures and in what ways do language policies (state-wide, nation-wide, institutional) become regulated socio-educational practices governing everyday [student and teacher] behavior? I begin addressing these questions by drawing on two excerpts from MacIntyre (1985: 187) wherein he defines and explains 'practice'. A practice is:

any coherent and complex form of *socially established cooperative human activity* through which *goods internal* to that form of activity are realized in the course of trying to achieve those which are appropriate to, and partially definitive of, that form of activity, with the result that human powers to achieve excellence, and *human conceptions of ends and goods involved are systematically extended*. (My emphasis)

Tic-tac-toe is not an example of a practice in this sense, nor is throwing a football with skill, but the game of football is, and so is chess. Bricklaying is not a practice, but architecture is. Planting turnips is not a practice, but farming is. So are the enquiries of physics, chemistry, and biology, and so is the work of the historian, and so are painting and music.

Tsoukas (1998) explains that there are four crucial features (corresponding to the italicized phrases in these two quotes) of a practice. First, a practice, as the previous definition points out, is a coherent, complex form of human activity, which means it is regulated by implicit and explicit rules and has been in existence for some time. In other words, a practice has a background to which it can be traced. Second, every practice establishes a set of *internal goods* that cannot be achieved in any other way but by participating in the practice itself. According to Tsoukas (1998), the kind of satisfaction gained from running a marathon, caring for sick patients or engaging in intensive research cannot be had without actively running, nursing or researching. (In contrast, 'external goods' such as prestige and wealth may be consequences of having participated in certain social practices but they are consequences that can be had by participating in others as well. In other words, external goods can be the result of a range of different social practices, whereas internal goods are particular to the practice to which they are associated [for a fuller discussion, see Tsoukas, 1998].)

Third, participating in a practice implies attempting to reach for the standards of excellence established by the regulators of the practice; i.e. each practice has its own criteria for gauging success. And fourth, every practice has its own history 'which is not only the history of the changes of technical skills relevant to a practice, but also a history of changes of the relevant ends to which the technical skills are put' (Tsoukas, 1998: 55). It is this sense of tradition that prompts MacIntyre (1985: 194) to say that

> to enter into a practice is to enter into a relationship not only with its contemporary practioners, but also with those who have preceded us in the practice, particularly those whose achievements extended the reach of the practice to its present point. It is thus the achievement, and *a fortiori* the authority, of a tradition which I then confront and from which I have to learn.

In other words, each of us – as students, teachers, researchers, mentors – find ourselves negotiating with the history of a practice, with ways in which the practice *preceded us*, with the *authority* of a tradition. It is this *preceding authority* (see previous quote) that is, among other things, inherently ideological and manifests itself as social practices. Toward explicating these abstract points, I turn now to addressing specific anti-English ideological movements before discussing the ways in which they became translated into socio-educational practices (including language policies). This discussion will also help us partially trace the historical roots of the English–Vernacular chasm.

Two Linked-Yet-Separate Anti-English, Pro-Vernacular Ideologies: Gandhi and the Remove English Lobby

This section addresses the pro-Vernacular ideological influences of Gandhi (particularly pertinent to the local realities covered in this book, since he was from the state of Gujarat) and the *Angrezi Hataao Aandolan (Remove English Lobby*, [hereafter *REL*], which lobbied to replace English with local Vernaculars). Both of these 'linked' ideologies (Ricento, 2000) were overlapping thought collectives, decidedly anti-English in their strains, stemming as they did from anti-British, pro-Independence sentiments, and have, in a variety of ways, contributed to the current educational scene in India, most notably by pitting one medium of instruction against the other.[1] Ideological influences such as these that shaped pro-Vernacular sentiments (especially after Independence when the country was devising its own rules for educational governance) undoubtedly made their way indirectly into the original National Education Policy (Ministry of Education, 1968), a treatise that first formally laid out the national language policies (Schiffman, 1996).[2] These policies are more or less still in place today and critically inform English and Vernacular education in institutions and classrooms across the country, in general, and Gujarat, in particular.

The Influence of Gandhi: anti-English, pro-Vernacular

Gandhi's views on English and the Vernaculars were closely allied with his struggles for Independence and were printed in *Harijan* and *Young India*, newspapers that carried his calls for Indian independence. Indeed, his call for national unity was integrally tied to encouraging all Indians to return to and enhance their Vernacular roots. This strong pro-Vernacular stance was most evident in his insistence that the Vernacular should be the medium of instruction for all children, an orientation that can be traced back to his retrospective account of his time in school, which emphasized English over Gujarati. The following quote effectively captures the 'barrier' English seemed to become:

> My head used to reel as the teacher was struggling to make his exposition on Geometry understood by us. I could make neither head nor tail of Geometry till we reached the 13th theorem of the first book of Euclid.

And let me confess to the reader that in spite of all my love for the mother-tongue, I do not to this day know the Gujarati equivalents of the technical terms of Geometry, Algebra and the like. I know that what I took four years to learn of Arithmetic, Geometry, Algebra, Chemistry, and Astronomy, I should have learnt easily in one year, if I had not to learn them through English but Gujarati. (Gandhi, 1954: 4–5)

Gandhi's ambivalence about English seemed to stem from his views about it being not only a 'borrowed' language that co-existed uneasily with local, indigenous languages, customs and lifestyles but one that threatened the delicate, newly-acquired self-respect of the country. The following two quotes from Gandhi (1954) capture this.

I must not be understood to decry English or its noble literature. The columns of the *Harijan* are sufficient evidence of my love of English. But the nobility of its literature cannot avail the Indian nation any more than the temperate climate or the scenery of England can avail her. India has to flourish in her own climate, and scenery and her own literature, even though all the three may be inferior to the English climate, scenery and literature. We and our children must build our own heritage. If we borrow another we impoverish our own. We can never grow on foreign victuals. (p. 5)

Surely it is a self-demonstrated proposition that the youth of a nation cannot keep or establish a living contact with the masses unless their knowledge is received and assimilated through a medium understood by the people. Who can calculate the immeasurable loss sustained by the nation owing to thousands of its young men having been obliged to waste years in mastering a foreign language and its idiom, of which in their daily life they have the least use and in learning which they had to neglect their own mother-tongue and their own literature? (p. 13)

The fact that Gandhi's home state was Gujarat played a role in the language policy adopted by the state when it came into being with the dissolution of the old Bombay Presidency and the creation of the two states of Maharashtra and Gujarat (Gujarat came into existence in 1960). Gandhi's own attachment to his mother tongue of Gujarati, and his emphasis on non-European languages as a means of expressing nationalist sentiment went some way in shaping the policy of a state in which English has not been able to put down roots (as it did in, say, the Bengal or Madras Presidency [present day Tamil Nadu]). The reasons for what seems like the relatively superficial hold of English on Gujarati *litterateurs* and the educated public are not easy to unravel: despite English education in some parts of present-day Gujarat, there was not a 'westernized, Anglicized class of the kind found in Bengal, or a class of people who mastered the intricacies of the English language' (S. Ramanathan, 2002, personal communication). One reason may be the fact that large parts of present day Gujarat were princely states and not directly under British rule.[3] Hence, the British presence was not quite as pervasive or strong in Gujarat as in other parts of India that were British India.

When Gujarat was declared a state in 1960, its people enthusiastically took to Gujarati for official purposes and introduced it as a medium at the tertiary educational level in parallel with English. By 1965, all official communication was only in Gujarati. This led to a decline in the amount of English used in the public sphere and to a decline in performance in English examinations.[4] Indeed, Gujarat College, an old government college affiliated to the old Bombay Presidency (and one of its premier institutions), changed character as it 'Gujarati-fied' itself and a Jesuit institution (studied in depth in Chapter 6) became one of the better sites for English education in the state.

From its inception, Gujarat, as the foregoing sketch suggests, privileged the Vernacular over English. Gandhi's views regarding the value of the Vernacular – of providing all children the right to an education in their mother-tongue (or a closely allied language) – is partially reflected in the formal stance adopted by the National Policy on Education (Ministry of Education,1968) on language instruction in the country's schools (to be discussed in the next section). Gujarat's anti-English stance was evident in other local realms as well. Morarji Desai, a prominent politician from Gujarat, and Prime Minister for a brief period, was strongly anti-English. In addition, Gujarat University, when electing its Vice Chancellor, chose L.R. Desai, an academic of the nativist kind over Vikram Sarabhai, who stood for progressive, westernized education, and who was a Cambridge-educated scientist with an international reputation and the architect of India's Space Programme. Westernized models of education seemed to be unacceptable to 'Gandhian' educationists. This theme – of empowering average Indians with an education in a medium that they can relate to was picked up by the REL (Vaidik, 1973), which was vehemently pro-Vernacular. I consider this second pro-Vernacular/anti-English ideological force in the next section.

The Remove English Lobby (*Angrezi Hatao Andolan*)

While not Gujarat-based, the values of the REL resonated strongly with then pervasive sentiments in Gujarat [5] and was perhaps sweet music in this state. [6] What makes committees such as the REL interesting – apart from its strident anti-English, pro-Vernacular sentiments – are its written documents which partially capture some of their key tenets. The very fact that formal documents were put together and formally published by this lobby points partially to the relative seriousness of the movement. One (original) document produced by this committee is in Hindi (published in 1973) and is about 46 pages long: I have, for the purposes of this chapter, picked out and translated those sections that best capture their stance and views on English.

(1) Making English compulsory [in Indian schools] has rendered hundreds of thousands of children handicapped. About 2% of the country's population has control over the country's resources through English. There appears to be only darkness for thousands of poor, oppressed villagers.... . (p. 1)

(2) English has divided Indians from other Indians. Because of English, there is in the country a small élite that looks down on the common person. Through English, one big part of this country remains weak and poor, and a very small portion rich. This was begun by the British and continues, appallingly, to this day. The removal of English is a matter of cultural and civic pride. Without removing English, we cannot eradicate poverty. (p. 2)

(3) Those who believe that English is an international language also believe that the world's knowledge is produced only in English, whereas in reality there are all kinds of domains in which progress has been made in a range of other languages. We either remain in ignorance of this knowledge or read about it only when it is translated into English. (p. 5)

(4) The country that wishes to keep all its doors open to the world must also keep all its windows open, not just the window of English. Keeping only the window of English open does not behoove us. Does a well-planned house have only one window? No, it has several from which winds from different directions can blow through. If there is a stench from one window, you have the option of opening other windows. But the well-established language institutions in this country seem to have made only one window. Whether there emnates a fragrance or a stench from this window, whether it overlooks a beautiful scene or an ugly one, it is the only one that is allowed to stay open. (p. 7)

(5) Goals of the committee:
  • to remove English and English influence in all domains of everyday life;
  • to resist making English mandatory in law courts, educational

institutions, and other important areas;
- to replace English with Indian languages;
- to establish such a community/society whereby the poorest of persons can reach the highest of social positions through the medium of his/her Vernacular. (p. 46)
(Translated by the author from Vaidik, 1973)

These segments are intended to demonstrate the general drift of some of the arguments proposed by the anti-English lobbyists. In Excerpts 1 and 2, the popularity of English is seen as an élitist phenomenon that separates Indians, in Excerpts 3 and 4, it is pitted against other languages with power flowing disproportionately between them, while Excerpt 5 partially formalizes that English–Vernacular dichotomy explicitly ('to replace English with Indian languages'). The overall motivation of the Committee – as the last goal of Excerpt 5 indicates – was to empower the masses by enhancing the Vernacular so that they, too, could strive for high social positions. In other words, the VM was to be the foundational rung of the social ladder. According to Chatterjee (1992: 302), English at this time was not considered desirable for the following reasons:

(1) it is a negation of democracy because it divides the Indian people into two nations: the few who govern, and the many who are governed; and
(2) it is educationally unsound to use a foreign language' .

Indeed, the University Education Commission of 1948–49 (see Appendix 2) along with REL movements formalized aspects of the English–Vernacular chasm which are now cemented in specific national- and state-wide socio-educational policies.

One key language-related policy that emerged from this schism was the Eighth Schedule in the Indian constitution, a policy that insists that all Indian children (up to the age of 14) have access to free education in one of India's 15 major languages (Gupta *et al.,* 1995). Idealistic as this vision was and still is – given India's multilingual ethos – the current place that the Vernacular and the VM student in Gujarat occupies is not that simple (Gargesh, 1995; Hasnain, 1995; Pattanayak, 1990).[7] S/he is situated in an area where the country's official languages are English and Hindi, where the state's policy has a distinct Gujarati bias and where, on the globalizing ground, English *appears* to be a powerful 'en-voicing' instrument. From some angles, the VM student now finds her/himself paying the price for a language policy that leaves her/him disadvantaged vis-à-vis her/his counterparts in other Indian states. From other angles, though, we see ways in which s/he attempts to integrate her/his Vernacular traditions critically with her ambitions to 'move ahead' (SI, 5: 1). As we will see in the following sections and the remainder of this book, attempting to understand some local ways in which English and the Vernaculars are embedded in social stratifications helps us see that much of what passes for literacy in the classroom goes on in 'peripheral' contexts outside it (Holliday, 1994; Street, 2002).

(Re)Tracing Our Steps: Understanding the Current English—Vernacular Chasm by Looking Back at Colonial Language Policies

Moving away from ideologies to addressing language policies, it might be useful (at the risk of being hugely simplistic) briefly to step further back into pre-Independence India to discuss how past colonial rulings and current postcolonial policies established an English–Vernacular dialectic that eventually solidified into particular socio-educational practices. As I mentioned in Chapter 1, I address colonial practices more by way of providing a historical perspective to some postcolonial realities. Because my overall focus is more on the postcolonial this section is, at best, a crude sketch. (For a comprehensive review, see Guha [1997] and Pennycook [1998].)

The spread of the British Raj and the English language went hand-in-hand. According to Khilnani (1998: 22), a big concern for the Raj was maintaining order and the British authorities could not do this solely by preserving the peace simply through coercion or even by the deft manipulation of interests. Instead, because it had to shape opinion, they began to cultivate a local élite who could understand them and their concepts of rule, who were willing to be inducted into politics, into a 'public arena', where they would freely give allegiance and loyalty to the British crown…'.

The following quote, cited in Pennycook (1998), sums up how English won out:

> It stands pre-eminent even among the languages of the West…Whoever knows that language has already access to all the vast intellectual wealth which all the wisest nations of the earth have created and hoarded in the course of ninety generations. It may safely be said that the literature now extant in that language is of greater value than all the literature which three hundred years was extant in all the languages of the world together. Nor is this all. In India, English is the language spoken by the ruling class. It is spoken by the higher class of natives at the seats of Government. It is likely to become the language of commerce throughout the seas of the East. (Bureau of Education, 1920: 110, cited in Pennycook, 1998: 80)

This need on the part of the Raj bears the early seeds of the English–Vernacular schism. Indeed, the general emphasis on teaching English literature instead of the language (as we shall see in Chapters 5 and 6) can be traced back to the need to produce an Indian gentry that reflected the then current British values, mores and world views so as to enable them to control their empire better (Rajan, 1992; Vishwanathan, 1989).

According to Agarwal (1984), this self-conscious cultivation of an Indian gentry (*English babus*, as they were called) was brought about by at least three over-cited colonial measures that influenced the (current) Indian educational system (see Appendix 2 for a breakdown of important educa-tion-related measures):

(1)   the East India Company was compelled to accept responsibility for the education of Indians in 1813;
(2)   Macaulay's infamous Minute (on 2 February 1835) wherein he denounced educating Indians in their mother tongue and upheld the intrinsic value of the English language and literature; and
(3)   Charles Wood's Dispatch of 1854 (see Appendix 2) which imposed on the government the 'task of creating a properly articulated scheme of education from primary school to the university' (Agarwal, 1984).

The system of education that the British introduced in India was modeled on the British system, especially in regard to higher education, and the striking feature of this educational transplantation was English, which was not only taught as a language but also became a medium of instruction (Jayaram, 1993). Indeed, the emphasis on mastering the English language in schools and colleges became so firmly entrenched and continues to assume such importance that some scholars believe it has 'encouraged mechanical learning through memorizing and discouraged inquisitiveness and an experimental bent of mind' (Jayaram, 1993: 85). This transplantion of the colonizer's educational system to meet a need in the colonies was the first step in establishing an English *versus* Vernacular socio-educational apparatus, a system that, before long, took on a life of its own and came up with its own language policies, which have become social practices. It is this postcolonial apparatus – a combination of colonial legacy and postcolonial practice – and the divisive role of English in this landscape that I am obsessed with.

Current Language Policies

In 1968, the Ministry of Education issued its National Policy on Education, wherein it specified its overall goals: a 'transformation of the system to relate it more closely to the life of the people; a continuous effort to expand educational opportunity; a sustained and intensive effort to raise the quality of education at all stages…' (Ministry of Education, 1968: 2). One key area of development in this statement dealt with regional languages.

The energetic development of Indian languages and literature is a *sine qua non* for educational and cultural development. Unless this is done, the creative energies of the people will not be released, standards of education will not improve, knowledge will not spread to the people, and the gulf between the intelligentsia and the masses will remain, if not widen further…. (p. 3)

This policy has generated some controversy about what the 'appropriate' mediums of instruction should be at both K–12 and beyond (Ageira, 1996; Jayaram, 1993). One area of general consensus has been that students opting to be educated in English take the Vernacular language as a second-language requirement, while students opting to be educated in the Vernacular have English as a second language. In either case, the foreign language is typically introduced in grade 5.

At the tertiary level, however, the implementation does not seem to be consistent and messages that students receive regarding the devaluation of their home Vernaculars seem consistent and systematic, coming as they do in varying, interconnected ways (Waseem, 1995; Khubchandani, 1995). For one, English appears to be the dominant medium of instruction across the Board.[8] This privileging of English as the medium of college instruction appears to preordain a self-perpetuating language/medium-related exclusivity. Students schooled in the Vernacular in the K–12 years – typically lower-income children – are often shut out of EM colleges, since their proficiency in English is generally considered to be poor. They end up in VM colleges, which typically only offer arts and commerce degrees. Most science and professionally related subjects – engineering, medicine, pharmacy, computer science – are typically offered only in English. This breakdown – where arts subjects are considered 'lower-level' and the sciences 'upper-level' disciplines – seems to dovetail with the language/medium in which they are taught, which in turn seems to dovetail with the class background of students. Middle-class, EM students have easier access to EM colleges and, thus, to all disciplines. Lower-income VM students who, because of their relative lack of fluency in English, (compared to their EM counterparts), have access only to 'lower-level' disciplines which, as this book will point out, do not get them the jobs they seek or the social standing they desire. It is in this intricate way that current language policies around English (as a medium of instruction) play crucial roles both in maintaining the *status quo* with the middle class and in perpetuating the English–Vernacular divide. Needless to say, by validating the role of English as much as it does at the tertiary realm and beyond, the general socio-educational apparatus is also simultaneously sending out implicit messages about the generally low regard it has for the Vernaculars both within the apparatus as a medium of instruction and in the larger social world to which the apparatus is inextricably tied.

Language policies and the ideologies generated by them together with other local factors on the ground sustain the larger socio-educational system (Spolsky, 1986; Ager, 2001). Together they have become reified into social practices and it would be worthwhile at this point to address briefly how this may have come about keeping Tsoukas' (1998) previously discussed criteria in mind. Language policies and ideologies, as the preceding discussion has pointed out, contribute to implicit and explicit rules that organize human activity and thought, including how students are channeled, in particular, in invisible grooves deemed 'appropriate' by the larger socio-educational apparatus. Some ways in which these practices cluster with other local factors are discussed in Chapters 4–6, which partially show the (divergent) internal goods that EM and VM students can achieve only if they participate in the general apparatus, including participating in gate-keeping procedures that govern standards of excellence established at state and institutional levels. These local factors seem distinctly pro-English: they position VM students in unfair competition with their EM counterparts and they do so by assuming a mantle of legitimacy.

In addition, these practices and the ways in which they find partial articulation in institutions, classrooms and teacher and student behaviors have, with repeated enactment, established a history to a point where a newcomer entering the socio-educational apparatus enters 'into a relationship not only with its contemporary practioners, but also with those who have preceded [us] in the practice' (MacIntyre, 1985: 194). Needless to say, VM students entering the college scene are often seen as entering 'too late' to engage fully with contemporary practitioners. These students have been, in most cases, incompletely socialized into the 'appropriate' powerful cultural models that EM students have received and endlessly rehearsed. Socialized as they have been to alternate models of literacy, these students find that their Vernacular ways of learning are not valued, especially in EM settings. It is against such a landscape that resistance perspectives need to be understood. The local efforts of teachers, administrators and institutions to find ways of integrating and en-voicing the Vernacular with English-dominant policies and practices and to adopt critical stances toward their everyday realities have to be placed against a system that is largely oriented to maintaining the English–Vernacular chasm.

The Larger Apparatus and the *Assumptions Nexus*

Implied in the previous discussion is the idea that a social practice becomes one when aspects of the social world are conducive to it being so. What must the social world be like for EM or VM knowledge production and consumption to be possible? Clearly, in order for social practices to operate, the social world must, to some extent, be regularized, patterned and non-random (Tsoukas, 1998). Berger and Luckmann (1966: 70) sum up the ordered character of reality as follows:

> All human activity is subject to habitualization. Any action that is repeated frequently becomes cast into a pattern, which can then be reproduced with an economy of effort and which, *ipso facto*, is appre-hended by its performer *as* that pattern. Habitualization further implies that the action may be performed again in the future in the same manner and with the same economical effort. (My emphasis)

'Habitualization' of 'educational activity' both produces and is an outcome of several social cogs aligning together in particular ways that seem actively to envoice one group over others because power flows in and between the ridges and cavities of all the cogs of this aligned socio-educational system (Ramanathan, 2002a). Speaking of alignment in a general sense, Wartenberg (1990, cited by Rouse, 1994) states:

> A field of social agents can constitute an alignment in regard to a social agent if and only if, first of all, *their actions in regard to that agent are coordinated in a specific manner.* To be in alignment, however, the coordinated practices of these social agents need to be comprehensive enough that the social agent facing the alignment encounters that alignment as *having control over certain things that she might either need or desire*...The concept of a social alignment thus provides a way of understanding the 'field' that constitutes a situated power relationship as a power relationship. (My emphasis)

The two highlighted phrases in this quote are crucial to the present discussion of the English–Vernacular dichotomy. The excerpt calls attention to societal structures being 'coordinated' and interlocked (as language policies, regulations, institutional practices and pedagogic materials are): they also point to how the alignment of various social cogs exercises control over the 'social agent' (including institutions, teachers and students). Habitualized human activity channels social agents to fit this aligned complex system that, in the present case, can be seen to have the English–Vernacular chasm at its core. This interlocking, aligned apparatus dovetails with the values and aspirations of the largely middle class to form an *assumptions nexus* that, in the present case, leaves VM students out of its pale. This phrase – *assumptions nexus* – is intended to capture the vast array of class-based social practices both inside and outside the home that privilege the middle class and that by its very existence subordinate low-income groups. The term includes everything in class-related conventions that inform how and why particular class groups live and make the choices they do in almost every realm of everyday existence, including those related to schooling, child-rearing, literacy practices at home, clothing and public appearances, food, how money gets spent, body sizes, weight, health, nutrition and hairdos and, most importantly, in the present case, opting for fluency in English (sometimes through an EM education). Only a very partial list, these outward manifestations of behavior are based on and indicative of a range of *assumptions that partially explain why things are the way they are* (and that, as this book repeatedly underscores, needs to be questioned and openly resisted). Over time, this nexus, comprised partly of the general educational apparatus and class-related assumptions, values and conventions assumes 'naturalized' overtones and exerts hegemonic influences. Williams (1977), writing about the relationship between hegemony and control of cultural resources, points out specific kinds of roles played by educational institutions in sustaining hegemonic ideologies. The following extended quote captures the crux of 'how the assemblage of meanings and practices leads to, and comes from, unequal economic and cultural control' (Apple, 1990: 5):

> [Hegemony] is a whole body of practices and expectations... . It is a set of meanings and values which as they are experienced as practices appear as reciprocally confirming. It, thus, constitutes a sense of reality... . We can understand a ... culture if we understand the real social process on which it depends: I mean the process of incorporation. The modes of incorporation are of great significance, and incidentally in our kind of society have a considerable economic significance. The educational institutions are usually the main agencies of transmission of an effective dominant culture... [A]t a philosophical level ... there is a process which I call the *selective tradition*...the way in which from a whole possible area of past and present, certain meanings and practices are neglected and excluded. Even more crucially, some of these meanings are reinterpreted, diluted, or put into forms which support or at least do not contradict other elements within the effective dominant culture. (My emphasis)

Identifying and exploring how some of the social cogs in the larger socio-educational system connect with each other to produce particular systematic consequences – over generations of students in this case – allows us to see how power (read 'English') circulates through the 'system' and is distributed across a range of social networks, thus producing a *selective tradition* that actively *dilutes* Vernaculars and Vernacular ways of knowing, learning and teaching. As we will see in the course of the book, language policies and latent ideologies form the backdrop against which all the other key educational sites, including pedagogic materials, teaching practices, gate-keeping examinations and teacher–student interactions can be understood: they also allow us to see how over time these practices, by becoming habitualized and systematic, slot students into invisible grooves. Exploring where some of these grooves are and the ways in which they lie hidden allows to begin to see where and how chasms around English and Vernacular knowledge are both produced and consumed, resisted and bridged, since domination and opposition, gulfs and bridges, are always parts of each other. English, from some lenses, divides.

Notes

1.   As will be evident, English and the Vernaculars were pitted against each other formally at least 55 years ago (at the time of Independence) and informally for years before that. The polarization that we see between them today is not new by any means.

2.   Rajiv Gandhi's Operation Blackboard scheme – like the National Policy on Education – also offered free education to children up to the age of 14. Developed in 1987, it targeted at least the following areas for improvement:
      •   Extensive teacher education
      •   Making provisions for: (1) at least one room for each class/section, (2) Headmaster-cum office room, (3) separate toilet facilities for girls and boys, (4) essential learning equipment including a library, (5) at least one teacher for each class/section and (6) a contingency grant for the replenishment of items, consumable and minor repairs, etc.
      •   Replacment of equipment
      •   Ensuring that at least 50% of the teachers appointed will be women.
      •   Low cost and locally available designs relevant to the local conditions will be adopted for school buildings.
      (On WWW at http://www. Arunmehta.freeyellow.com/page72.html)
      An ambitious scheme, Operation Blackboard was ultimately regarded as flawed.

3.   There would, however, be a British resident at the courts.

4.   This was an issue discussed in several newspapers that have recently reported the performance of different states in the All India Civil Service examinations (conducted until very recently only in English). Candidates from Gujarat, apparently, seldom made the grade.

5.   In fact, Gujarat's lack of proficiency in English was a subject of jokes in other states. The now defunct weekly *Current,* edited by Dr F. Karaka, ran a column

showing two Gujaratis, dressed in typical Gujarati attire, wearing dhotis and Gandhi caps, standing at a bus stop and talking in less than fluent English. Every column ended with 'Boycott British language!' (a clear reference to Gandhi's Boycott British Goods campaign).

6. But in fact, it was about this time that Gujarat was waking up to the fact that the general performance of Gujaratis – in national examinations for the Indian Civil Service or the Indian Administrative Service – were not favorable (as compared to those of other states) and that one reason for this was their language policies.

7. Gargesh (1995: 86) maintains that 'layers of disadvantage, with respect to language, are in the order of
   (a) English, as opposed to Indian languages
   (b) English and Hindi as opposed to other Scheduled Indian languages,
   (c) English, Scheduled languages with state as opposed to stateless languages and
   (d) English and Scheduled languages as opposed to non-Scheduled languages.'

8. According to Jayaram (1993), a little more than half of the universities offer bilingual instruction in one or more courses, with English being one of the mediums of instruction. Only 13 of the 97 centralized universities (all colleges in India are affiliated to specific central universities in the various states) listed in *The Universities Handbook* appear to offer multilingual media of instruction.

Chapter 3

Divisive and Divergent Pedagogical Tools for Vernacular- and English-medium Students

Anandbhai is Sumeet's uncle. He is showing a book to Sumeet. This book is an encyclopedia.

Sumeet: *Look at this picture, uncle. Who are these people in the street?*
Uncle: *They are Chinese men and women.*
Sumeet: *Why are they beating drums? Why are they shouting?*
Uncle: *Wait a little. Look at the picture again. What else do you see?*
Sumeet: *Well, this is either the sun or the moon.*
Uncle: *It is the sun.*
Sumeet: *But we can't see the whole of it. A part of it is dark.*
Uncle: *Why is it dark? Can you tell me?*
Sumeet: *Is it because there is a solar eclipse?*
Uncle: *You are right.*
Sumeet: *But why are these people beating drums and shouting?*
Uncle: *Look! In old days people believed in strange things. In China people said, 'The solar eclipse occurs because a huge dragon tries to swallow the sun!' So they came out of their houses. They beat the drums and made a lot of noise. They said, 'We'll make a noise and the dragon will run away.'*
Sumeet: *That is very strange.*
Uncle: *Yes, it is. In some European countries too people had a similar belief. They said, 'The solar eclipse occurs because two big wolves try to swallow the sun.'* **In India too there was such a belief. People said, 'A solar eclipse occurs because Rahu swallows the sun. A lunar eclipse occurs because Ketu swallows the sun.'**
Sumeet: *But Uncle, how does an eclipse really take place? What do scientists say?*
Uncle: *That is a really good question. The reason is this: The earth moves around the sun and the moon around the earth....Sometimes the moon gets between the sun and the earth. Since the shadow of the moon hides*

a part of the sun, that part of the sun appears dark. That is the solar eclipse. (Kotak *et al.*, 1999: 91–2) An English language textbook used in the VM, grade 7; my emphasis)

To what extent are (English) language textbooks pedagogical artifacts that can be studied in isolation from their social, political, institutional and cultural environments? Should they be viewed as part of a larger system of socio-literate practices serving as conduits that transfer selected cultural values and norms? Or should they be viewed as key sites of 'cultural and epistemological invasion, where inappropriate and irrelevant forms of Western culture and knowledge are thrust upon an unwitting student population?' (Pennycook, 1996: 64). The previous excerpt from an English textbook used in VM teaching makes several related points, including the relatively obvious one regarding the high degree of nativization in textbooks where English has been appropriated into local contexts, infused with local names and amalgamated with local ways of explaining, among other things, eclipses. A somewhat less obvious point in the excerpt is the idea that the 'English/scientific' way of explaining eclipses is presented as the 'correct' way. The correlation between 'English', 'scientific' and 'correct', on the one hand, and 'non-English' and 'strange', on the other, and the generally 'de-voicing' message this combination of phrases sends out to non-English/VM students and teachers cannot be missed.

Questions and issues such as these motivate my exploration of English-language textbooks used in both Gujarati- and English-medium K–12 schools in Gujarat. To gain a better understanding of some of the ways in which these students are partially socialized before arriving at the college scene, I decided to purchase and critically review the key English language textbooks used for both sets of students. The sense I have made of these books and the interpretation that I offer of them here have to be understood in the context of the two divergent institutions that I explore in the next chapter. As one that was schooled in the EM, some of the English language textbooks examined here are similar to those in which I was schooled. As I discovered during my forays into the worlds of VM and EM students and teachers, a reason for the English–Vernacular divide is partially tied to the cultural models into which the two different student populations are socialized. I did not realize how much of an 'outsider' I was in my own native city, until I began to realize that my (EM) cultural models were markedly different from other (VM) Ahmedabadis, with divergent views regarding what it means to be 'literate in English'. As I am hoping to show, the divergent cultural models of both sets of students are embedded in a complex syndrome of issues including those related to English language learning and teaching, inter-relations between English and India's numerous co-existing indigenous/Vernacular languages, practices associated with Vernacular language teaching/learning, particular state- and nation-wide educational policies, institutional mandates about which language(s) get(s) used in (English) language classrooms, as well as latent generalized views about the general superiority of English over other local languages. Viewing these textbooks as 'cultural artifacts' that are embedded in this aligned multifaceted scene, their divergent forms and content draw on and promote very distinct cultural models regarding English language literacy, models that are habitualized into social practices that continuously feed and sustain inequalities between student populations. The resistance efforts detailed in Chapters 5 and 6, which address the Vernacular–English divide at the tertiary level, need to be partially appreciated in the light of what both sets of students bring with them. The simultaneously divisive and de-voicing role that English literacy plays in this should not be under-estimated. As with Chapter 2, the voice I am adopting here is relatively more distant because I want to focus primarily on the textbooks: I will make occasional reference to my own EM cultural models where relevant.

I noted earlier that college-level 'professional' degrees (computer science, engineering, the hard sciences, pharmacy and medicine) in India are generally offered only in English and that students schooled in the VM find themselves seriously disadvantaged at the tertiary level because their English proficiency at the end of the 12th grade is gener-ally deemed to be inadequate for college-level work. Added to this is the complicating university mandate that insists that all VM and EM students take the same 'English compulsory' examination in their third and final year of college. To gain a partial understanding of why VM students struggle the way they do at the tertiary level, this chapter attempts to explore the kind of English language teaching and learning practices to which these students have been acclimatized in their K–12 years. The textbooks under investigation are state-mandated books used in all VM and EM K–12 public schools in Gujarat. Teachers in all public schools have to use these primary materials in accordance with prescribed state-regulated syllabi and all formal assessments (examina-tions, tests, graded assignments) are based on students' grasp of the material covered in these textbooks. Each grade for both Gujarati and English classes has one primary English text and it is this set of texts that forms the heart of this chapter. Because VM students have to take English as a second language from grades 5 (when it is introduced) through 12, I analysed the primary English language textbooks for these grades.[1] Likewise, I analysed the relevant primary English language textbooks texts used in EM classes as well. As we will presently see, the two sets of textbooks are significantly divergent from each other, differences that have crucial implications when the two sets of students arrive at the college scene.

Cultural Models

Notional and fuzzy, the term 'cultural models' is hard to pin down. Cultural models, as the following brief discussion indicates, partially inform our respective 'takes'/slants/orientations to all of the things in the world. Shore (1996: 44) believes that 'cultural models' refer to 'an extensive and heterogenous collection of "models" that exist both as public artifacts "in the world" and as cognitive constructs "in the minds" of members of a community' (Shore, 1996: 44). In as much as cultural models are actual material and public artifacts, they are tangibly available in the world. Thus, objects such as houses, pottery, paintings, types of clothing, songs and textbooks are visible representations of particular cultural models. But cultural models can also be less visible and intersubjectively shared by a cultural group (D'Andrade, 1990: 809) and can be 'instituted' or 'personal', capturing as they do 'images or storylines or descriptions of simplified worlds in which prototypical events unfold' (Gee, 1999: 59).

Lines between personal and public/instituted cultural models are hard to draw, and there are contexts in which there is much overlap between them.[2] The fact that I ring the temple bell as I enter a Hindu temple in India or that I remove my shoes when I enter someone's house are 'automatic' gestures I follow when I am operating in particular contexts in that cultural context. These are conventionalized public models (with some visible aspects) that I have internalized. However, there need not always be a direct line from the transmission of these models to their direct assimilation and internalization. Transmission is more complicated because the social order is so. If there were, indeed, a one-to-one correspondence between cultural models and our assimilation of them, 'there would be no need to study how social messages are appropriated by individual minds' (Strauss, 1992).

Models typically become institutionalized when they are available as public forms by which individuals get socialized (Berger & Luckman, 1966). The more obvious instances of institutionalized cultural models are performance genres like dancing, games and ritual practices which become 'framed' by particular, accompanying motions: the rising of the curtain and lowering of lights in an auditorium before the beginning of a dance performance, for instance. Both sets of textbooks examined in this chapter are public forms that reflect instituted models that perpetuate 'detachable' literacy events: as we will presently see, these texts frame language learning

– reading and writing primarily – in a series of co-occurring, patterned, albeit divergent ways.

A Partial Historical Sketch: Textbook Culture, Examinationins and Bureaucratic Control – Vestiges of a Colonial Past

While there have been a range of postcolonial measures related to education in the Indian educational scene, there are pockets in the landscape that reflect colonial vestiges and the domain of textbooks and its pervasive influence is one of them. In his discussion of the dominant 'textbook culture' in the Indian educational system, Kumar (1987) believes that the current privileged place that textbooks occupy can be traced back to the 19th century during the Raj when several educational policies and practices were set in motion (see Appendix 2 for a list of historical dates marking enforcements of particular educational policies [Ageira, 1996; Chatterjee, 1992]), thereby ensuring the textbooks' dominant position. Because the prevailing sentiment at the time was that the Raj seemed to need a class of Indians that were Indian in colour and blood but English in tastes, opinions, morals and intellect (Macaulay in his 1835 Education Minute, see Appendix 2), the British administration set in motion an ideology that basically deemed local curricula and materials to be unsuitable for the type of office jobs they had in mind. The indigenous curriculum was considered inappropriate for another reason as well which was that it failed to work on the Indian character and morals which would bring it into line with Victorian ideals and values.[3] 'The new perception assigned an important role to education, that of 'molding Indian character by introducing children and their teachers to the English culture, history, and ethics' (Kumar, 1987: 14). The introduction of English as the language of change transfigured Indian public life. 'It obviously divided the British rulers from their Indian subjects; and it also divided Indians themselves, between those who could speak English, who knew their Dicey from their Dickens, and those who did not' (Khilnani, 1998). Coupled with English, then, textbooks, along with new curricular materials, became and, to some extent, have remained instruments for colonial imposition (Jawaare, 1998). The following are some features of the educational policies that were set in motion:

(1) The reformed educational system would be aimed at Europeanizing children and youth in both attitudes and perceptions. It will aim at 'imparting to them skills required for working in colonial administration, particularly at its middle and lower rungs' (Kumar, 1987:14).

(2) English language teaching and its use as a medium of instruction would be a means of this acculturation.

(3) Local, indigenous schools would have to conform to the syllabus and textbooks if they wished for financial assistance.

(4) The new system would be held in place by a centralized bureaucratic system that would oversee at every stage all aspects of the educational system, including syllabi, curricular materials, examination policies, teacher-training and, of course, textbooks.

All four of these mandates seem to have remained (with little change) in the current Indian educational system placing teachers in positions with little autonomy or influence over the pacing and ordering of knowledge, an issue that was brought up time and again by the teachers. State Boards of Education prescribe textbooks across the state for each subject and teachers are generally expected to teach them in a predetermined order.

She must ensure that all lessons are finished and preferably rehearsed, before the end of the school year, and that children are able to write answers to questions based on any lesson in the textbook without seeing it, for this is what they will have to do in the examination when they face one. (Kumar, 1987: 3)

Coupled with this reliance on textbooks are two other factors holding the textbook culture in place: (1) a general paucity of materials other than textbooks and (2) mandatory assessments during each year, with examinations being based on textbooks (Kumar, 1987). In my own experience, as one going through the EM track, I grew up believing that the textbook was to be the primary source of what I was to be tested on. As for the 'examination culture', I would have to say it occupied a very central role: I vividly recall spending weeks before examinations waking up at 3 o'clock in the morning to study. Teaching and learning all subjects – including (English) language/s – was and still seems to be oriented toward performance in formal (end-of-the year) examinations (Ramanathan, 1999).

Cultural Models in Textbooks

I mentioned earlier that the present analysis of textbooks is partially aimed at understanding some substantial differences in the ways in which English is presented and, consequentially, taught to both sets of students so as to understand the difficulties that VM students encounter at the college level better. As one of the quotes heading this chapter points out, textbooks are more than just 'delivery systems' of 'facts', published as they are within political and economic constraints of market, resources and power (Apple & Christian-Smith, 1991). Serving as more than just conduits, they draw on significantly divergent cultural models regarding 'being literate in English'.

While my presentation of these particular cultural models may, to some extent, come across as monolithic and static, it is not intended that way. Instead, I am trying to uncover larger, divergent systematized patterns of literacy practices on which the two sets of texts are based. This is not to say that local and sub-cultural differences within communities do not exist but that certain overarching social practices that fall along the lines of class and medium-of-instruction are at issue here. The types of questions that informed the analysis of these textbooks include the following ones.

(1) Which cultural models are at work here? In what ways are they evident? What kinds of cultural assumptions are they making in order for us to make sense of these texts and interact with them in 'appropriate' ways?

(2) Is there a gulf between what the textbooks espouse as 'appropriate' ways of learning and the actual practices they insist upon?

(3) What kinds of value judgements are being made about oneself or others? Are particular groups of people/particular behaviors being presented systematically in one way (positive or negative). What kind of message does such consistency seem to convey?

(4) To what other master models are the cultural models, as revealed in the texts, tied?

(5) What kinds of related cultural models – other literacy practices, the media, other learning experiences (at school or home), related institutions – play into/affect the cultural models in the textbooks?

(6) In what ways can the cultural models in the textbooks be seen to privilege one group of students over others? How do they do this? How do these cultural models work with others in the culture to perpetuate the gulf between the 'haves' and 'have-nots'? (Adapted from Gee, 1999: 78.)

Direct and indirect responses to these questions have guided the analysis offered here. I begin by briefly describing features common to both sets of texts. However, as we will see, the differences outweigh the commonalities both in terms of number and significance. Both the common features and the differences allow us to see how particular conventional 'detachable' models of English literacy have become public and institutionalized through a constant re-enactment and reproduction of certain socio-textual practices.

Features Common to Both Sets of Texts

There appear to be at least two overarching ways in which both sets of textbooks are similar: the first has to do with the (relatively common) idea that formal language learning is a developmental process and needs to be broken down into discrete, accessible units; and the second has to do with the notion that language textbooks are appropriate locations for passing on the wider democratic and secular values that students are expected to pick up in their language learning process.

(Formal) Language learning as a developmental process

Both sets of textbooks for grades 5–7 are laid out in terms of *minimal levels of learning* (MLL, see Appendix 3 for a grade-wise breakdown of English language proficiencies that are to be acquired), a concept that is partially explained in the opening pages of the texts as 'competencies that are determined keeping in mind the age and requirements of the students' (Gujarat State Board of Education, 1999: 1). Written primarily for teachers and parents, the MLL explanation lays out the different literacy skills that students are expected to have mastered by the end of any given year. All of the texts are built on incremental levels of difficulty, with more focus on 'basic' skills in the early grades and relatively 'difficult' skills being targeted from grade 8 onwards. (However, as Appendix 3 partially points out, the general breakdown of these skills in both sets of texts are very different, with markedly different competencies expected of Gujarati- and English-medium students.)

Texts as conduits for liberal values on secularism and multiculturalism and mutual respect

In keeping with one of the 'fundamental duties of every Indian citizen' listed in the opening pages of all of the textbooks ('to promote harmony …amongst all the people of India transcending religious, linguistic, and regional or sectional diversities; to renounce practices derogatory to the dignity of women…' [Gujarat State Board of School Textbooks, 1999: 3]), both sets of texts, at all levels, evidence marked secular attitudes, with lessons that have characters of different ethnic and religious backgrounds operating in congenial contexts. Thus, the English textbook for the VM in Grade 6 has conversations between characters called Meena, Abdul, Rupa and Hasan discussing how to buy train tickets and what they saw at the village fair: the readings in the EM textbooks likewise have characters that have Hindu, Muslim and Christian names.

At a superficial level, one could make the claim that these common features draw on and reify two common cultural models regarding English language learning. Latent beneath the first is that 'certain language-related features are easier to learn' and are, thus, to be taught in a certain order, a point that partially explains the division into 'basic' *versus* 'difficult' skills. Implicit in the second is the idea that language textbooks are vehicles by which to develop 'proper attitudes and perspectives…since the underpinnings of the course material have certain intrinsic values of life at their core…courage, self-help, spirit of adventure, mutual sympathy, and cooperation' (Gujarat State Board of School Textbooks, standard grade 6, 1998: iv). Pervasive as these cultural models are in all schools in the state of Gujarat, they can be seen to partially institutionalize certain beliefs about English language literacy in the Indian context, at least in regards to how it is to be taught and what is to be taught through it. However, the differences between the textbooks – certainly from my own EM point of view – seem stark enough to obliterate these common features.

Divergent Models of English Literacy in Gujarati- and English-medium Textbooks

There appear to be three central ways in which the Gujarati-medium (GM) English language textbooks differ from those used in EM classes and these differences have to do with (1) particular kinds of metadiscourse to students and/or teachers, (2) westernized teaching practices (or the lack of them) and (3) content of the readings.

Differences related to metadiscourse in textbooks

One area of noticeable difference has to do with the kind of instructions and metadiscourse to teachers and/or students of both sets of texts.[4] Metadiscourse is typically aimed at enhancing comprehension (by summarizing/paraphrasing content), critical reading (by identifying authors' attitudes/biases) and learning (remembering new information about subject matter, authors' attitudes and discourse strategies).

Metadiscourse: Instructions and explanations to teachers/students in translation in VM texts

The two sets of texts seem to evidence different kinds of metadiscourse, with the VM texts falling primarily toward the referential/informational end of the spectrum and the EM counterparts toward the expressive end. The VM texts for grades 5–7 evidence instructions/metadiscourse only in Gujarati to both teachers and students (I have provided the gloss); from grade 8 onwards, instructions in these texts are presented in both Gujarati and English. Figure 3.1 lays out samples of instructions/metadiscourse in the VM textbooks that occur at the end of readings (the italics and underlining are present in the texts.

V શિક્ષકો માટે :

1. આ પાઠ દ્વારા નીચેની ભાષાસામગ્રી શીખવવાની છે :

Teaching points	Examples
I am + name	I am Mona.
He/She is + name	He is Peter.
	She is Anita.

Structure words	Formulas
arm is	Hello !
he she	Good.
I	Thank you.

2. **સમજૂતી** : વાત કરતી વખતે બોલનાર વ્યક્તિ પોતાને માટે **I** વાપરે છે; બોલનાર કે સાંભળનાર સિવાયની ત્રીજી વ્યક્તિ વિશે વાત કરતાં તે છોકરો કે પુરુષ હોય તો **he** અને છોકરી કે સ્ત્રી હોય તો **she** વાપરે છે. **I**ની સાથે **am** તથા **he/she** સાથે **is** નો પ્રયોગ થાય છે અને પછી નામ મુકાય છે; જેમકે,

> I am Anil
> He is Vipul
> She is Renu

Figure 3.1 Metadiscourse in grade 5 GM texts (Nataraj & Joshi, 1999: 5)

[Gloss: When speaking, the speaker alone uses *I*; when speaking of a third person, both speaker and listener use *he* for a boy or a man and *she* for a girl or woman, as in I am Anil, He is Vipul, She is Renu).]

EXERCISES

1. You are telephoning your friend. Say, hello. Give your name.
    Then make sure that the other person is your friend. Your
    friend will answer. Work in pairs as shown below.

તમે તમારા મિત્રને ટેલિફોન કરો છો. પ્રથમ તમે કોણ છો તે જણાવશો. પછી સામી
વ્યક્તિ તમારો મિત્ર છે કે કેમ તેની ખાતરી કરશો. મિત્ર જવાબ આપશે. નીચે
જણાવ્યા પ્રમાણે બે-બેની જોડમાં વાતચીત કરો.

A : Hello ! I am ——— .
Are you ——— ?
Yes, I am ——— .

Figure 3.2 Metadiscourse in grade 8 GM texts (Kotak *et al.*, 1996: 10)

The detailed 'explanations' (*samjuti*) devoted to particular grammatical
points are evident in the textbooks for grades 5–7. The absence of them in
EM texts makes one wonder about latent assumptions being made of VM
(students and) teachers: that their English proficiency may not be adequate
and that they may need these detailed explanations. Also, all instructions
seem primarily referential in nature with authors discussing how the
language works: in the first excerpt, teachers and students are told how
pronouns+verbs work, while in the second, students are informed about
telephone etiquette in English. Instructions for teachers in EM texts work
quite differently. When they do occur, they typically have to do with
suggestions for being 'creative': developing exercises that foster students'
oral fluency with their writing skills, ways of teaching rhythm and
contrasting vowel sounds and ideas for bringing in topically related realia
(addressed presently).

Metadiscourse in EM texts: Authorial stances

Metadiscourse that indicates authorial stances/perspectives in the readings seem more evident in EM texts, and appears in summaries preceding each reading (short stories, essay, poems) in these texts. They are statements that not only indicate the author's orientation toward the reading but the orientation that the author hopes students will take. The following are examples of such statements from summaries (emphases in the original):

Grade 5: Little Bubli wanted to buy a gift for her mother. But she had only 3 rupees. What could she buy with three rupees? Though she bought a very small gift, her love and concern made the gift invaluable for her mother. (Jadeja *et al.*, 1999: 45)

Grade 6: Greg Raver Lampman knew that the terrible disease cancer could kill him very soon. So in a heroic and touching effort he began writing a series of sometimes hopeful, sometimes heartbreaking but always deeply moving letters to his little daughter he might never see growing up. This is one of those letters which have a message of hope and courage in the face of an ordeal. It urges us not to give up dreams, for without dreams life would be meaningless. (Purani *et al.*, 1998)

Grade 7: Mahatma Gandhi (1869–1948), the Father of the nation, who led our country to freedom from British rule, was also a prolific writer in more than one language. He wrote on a very wide range of topics in a style that was simple and yet effective. The lesson is an excerpt from his autobiography titled *My Experiments with Truth*, originally written in Gujarati as *Satyana Prayogo*. It tells us about the qualities of truthfulness and sincerity, which were a part of Gandhiji's character right from early years and were also reflected in his later life as a great leader of the people. (Purani *et al.*, 1999: 65)

Grade 8: Dr. Mulk Raj Anand, winner of a Sahitya Akademi Award, was born in Punjab in 1905...In the 30's Dr Anand was among the first writers to draw our attention to the poverty and destitution of the millions around us. It used to be bad taste to talk about such things in polite society then. The story that follows is an allegory. It has a hidden lesson to be learnt. The camel with his head up in the air is saved by a rat whose only home is a hole in the ground. (Thaker, 1999)

While not couched as overt instructions, the underlined statements in each of the previous summaries serve a metadiscoursal function by partially indicating the kind of slant the author wishes the students to take when reading the story. In each case, these summaries reflect some of the principles on which these texts are based: 'courage, self-help, spirit of adventure, mutual sympathy, and cooperation...'.[5] The excerpt from the grade 5 text directs students not to assess gifts in terms of their material worth, just as the excerpt from grade 8 conveys the idea that the 'lowliest' of people are of just as much 'value' as those higher up on the economic scale. Indeed, several of the comprehension-based questions at the end of the readings are geared toward students ferreting out relevant values-based information from the stories and for providing their opinions on the issue, thus enhancing their critical reading skills. The following are examples:

- Was it right of Andy to bring three letters instead of one? Give reasons.
- In what way is the world composed more of the past than the present?
- Who was their guide? How did he prove that he was strong?

The instructions/metadiscourse in both sets of textbooks, then, partially reveal assumptions made of EM *versus* VM students: the overall emphasis in VM texts on grammar and survival English (see Appendix 3 for the grade-wise breakdown of MLLs) and the contrasting emphasis in EM texts on addressing relatively complex reasoning about civic responsibility and human values is already laying the ground for the unequal tracking of professional opportunities to which the two sets of students will have access at tertiary levels of education. One set of students will have developed relatively sophisticated ways of reasoning in a language that is seen to be integrally tied to the society's social goods, while the other set of students will have not. While VM students are exposed to critical language tasks in their Gujarati classes – indeed all those interviewed said they had did not have much trouble with doing such work in Gujarati – it is in the realm of English that they seem to be most unfairly positioned. Not only are these some of the kinds of language tasks that they are called on to display later at the college level, they are also expected to compete with their EM counterparts in their third and final year by taking the same English examination. Needless to say, EM students, with years of rehearsal and practice behind them, find such tasks relatively easy.

Differences related to (lack of westernized) teaching practices: Self-learning, opinions, compositions, voice

Another realm of significant difference between the two sets of texts has to do with language-related exercises that seem to foster more 'individualistic' tendencies of EM students, and the absence of them in the VM counterparts (Atkinson, 2001; Ramanathan & Atkinson, 1999). The inclusion and rehearsal of these activities encourage EM, middle-class students to see themselves as individuals with opinions that matter and that need to be articulated. (The lack of them in VM texts, in contrast, makes one wonder about the implicitly conveyed sense of inappropriateness of these traits in VM students). Culled from EM texts, the two kinds of exercises at the end of readings that foster such qualities are those entitled 'self-learning' and 'compositions'.

Self-learning
    Related to themes in the readings and partially related to the exercises at the end of the readings, these sections are like miniature puzzles on which students are supposed to work on their own. The following sections of 'self-learning' are culled from the textbooks:

Grade 5:
[At the end of a reading on different seasons]
(1)   Make word-flowers for each season. Write the name of the season in the middle and words associated with it in the petals. One on summer is partly done for you. (From Jadeja *et al.*, 1999: 5)

(2)   Arrange the following events in proper order:
        Larry was in the next room doing his homework.
        Larry found the stamp from the 11th seat in row five.
        When Mr. Halperin was arrested, he whispered, 'Seven, Alice, like in the old clock.'
        Larry entered the theatre and went to the seat he wanted.
        Mr. Halperin had taken the stamp to help his wife.
        (From Jadeja *et al.,* 1999: 23)

Grade 6:
'E' is one of the commonest letters in the English language. Insert the letter 'E' in the following wherever required to make complete words:
    Examples NTR – ENTER
    AGL, CHS, HR, VRY, SVN, STM, THR, FL, NDL, KPR
    (Purani *et al.,* 1998: 68)

Grade 7
[Based on an excerpt from *The Diary of Anne Frank*]
We think of some human qualities as positive and some others as negative. For example, 'love' as we all agree, is a positive quality. Enter a tick in the appropriate column against each adjective given in the following table:

Quality	*Positive*	*Negative*

love
jealousy
courage
pride
tolerance
selfishness
cowardice
nobility
(Purani *et al.*, 1999: 130–1)

As such exercises are included in 'self-learning' sections, they seem to be based on the assumption that (EM) students will not need help with them, and will be able to accomplish these tasks on their own: seventh-grade children should be able to specify that jealousy and cowardice are 'negative' qualities, just as the fifth-grade students should be able to arrange jumbled narrative events in a particular, chronological order. The preface for the EM texts in grades 5–8 insist that 'self-learning is an essential part of the MLL approach' and that they

should be used for confidence-building as well as maximization of learning. The pupils should be...encouraged to do the work independently, and the outcomes of their efforts should be utilized for informal assessment (Gujarat State Board of School Textbooks, 1999: vi).

EM students are supposed to be 'confident' and to be able to 'work independently', behavioral traits that, interestingly, have no place in VM texts. Indeed, such divergent expectations do not just operate at an implicit level (as we will see in Chapter 5).

Opinions in compositions

EM texts also specifically ask their students to write about their opinions on certain topics in sections entitled 'composition'. The writing prompts in almost all the EM textbooks expect students to present/manipulate their 'voices' (Ramanathan, 2002a) to suit the topic. The following are representative samples from textbooks for grades 5–7:

Grade 5:
- Write a short paragraph of 10–12 on Madam Cama.
- Imagine you are Anabelle Nelson. Write a letter to Manisha saying how you celebrated the first anniversary of your friendship.
- Two boys go on a trip to the mountainside. They see a cave and go inside. To their great surprise, they find a treasure. As they are

coming out, they come face to face with the chief of the robbers...Now write 10–12 sentences to complete this story.
- If you could become invisible for a day, what would you do? Write about it 10–15 sentences. (Jadeja *et al.*, 1999)

Grade 6:
- Do you know a simple-minded person like Andy? Write ten sentences about him or her.
- Write two paragraphs about your plans for Christmas /Diwali/Id.
- You are traveling by bus/train. There is an accident on the way. Write two paragraphs describing your experience.
- Write an autobiography of a circus animal.
- Write a paragraph on 'if I were a bird...'
(Purani *et al.*, 1998)

Grade 7
- Write a short autobiography of a dog.
- Write a short essay on: My favorite bird.
- Write an essay on the migration of birds and some reasons for it.
- Imagine that you were lost in a strange place. Write about your experiences.
- Do you know the difference between a portrait and a photograph? A photograph only shows us how a person looked at a particular time. A portrait, too, tells us about a person's appearance, but in addition, it may reveal traits of a person's character, personality, habits, etc. Prepare a word portrait of a nurse or a traffic policeman.
(Purani *et al.*, 1999)

Several of these essay prompts ask students to assume another 'voice' – 'If I were a bird' ... or an autobiography of a circus animal, or being Annabelle Nelson – and articulate their views on them. While the notion of voice may not be overtly taught or emphasized as it sometimes is in writing/composition textbooks used in composition classes in North American universities, for instance (indeed, I do not remember the use of the term when I was going through school there [Ramanathan & Atkinson, 1999]), prompts such as these are asking students to put themselves in somebody else's position and write from that position. Writing tasks in VM texts, especially from grades 5–7 (as evident in the divergent MLLs; see Appendix 3) are limited to 'gaining control of the basic mechanics of writing like capital and small letters' (grade 5), to 'writing words and sentences neatly on a line with proper spacing' (grade 6), to writing 'answers to questions based on the text' (grade 7).[6] Sections entitled 'compositions' or exercises devoted to any kind of extended writing are conspicuously absent.

The general lack of sections on 'self-learning' and voicing one's opinions contributes to the larger sense of the divergent qualities the two sets of students should/should not be able to evidence with being literate in English. Almost all of the VM students in colleges – explored in depth in Chapters 4 and 5 – unequivocally maintained that they were perfectly comfortable voicing opinions and probing civic issues in Gujarati but felt that they had not been taught to do so in English. Unfortunately, the examinations that they have to pass at the college level seem to be heavily oriented toward EM cultural models.

Differences related to readings/content in the two sets of textbooks

The readings in both sets of texts point to divergent English literacy models as well. VM texts with their general focus on survival English emphasize how language is used in particular Indian contexts (at the park, at the zoo or sending a telegram). The readings in EM texts, in contrast, are more Anglo-focused, drawing as they do from British, American and Indian literary texts. Table 3.1 charts out partial lists of contents for grades 6, 8 and 10.

Several interesting features emerge from a close comparison of the content in the two sets of textbooks. Poetry, a genre that draws heavily on the metaphorical use of language, is relegated to the 'optional' category in VM texts. Indeed, prefaces to the textbooks say that poetry, for VM students, is to be regarded as 'supplementary reading'. EM texts, in contrast, include essays and short readings from a relatively panoramic range of texts, with readings on Abraham Lincoln in grade 6, to those by Stephen Leacock and Tolstoy in grade 8, to ones by Hemmingway and Tagore in Grade 10. Also, poetry is not an optional category in these texts.

Other interesting details related to content also emerge: none of the prose sections in the VM texts (which generally comprise most of the text) are identified by the authors who wrote them, giving the impression that because these pieces are not 'creative' and literary, they do not need to be author-identified. Also, the cover pages of these (VM) texts have very local, Indian scenes: Indian kids chasing butterflies and birds (grades 5 and 6), Indian kids reading (grades 7 and 8), Indian fishermen rowing boats, lions in Gir Forest (grade 10), a Kathakali dancer in costume (grade 11). EM texts, in contrast, have a more westernized slant with portraits of Shakespeare (grade 7), Tagore and Shakespeare (grade 8), Sarojini Naidu and Charles

Table 3.1 List of contents for grades 6, 8 and 10

	GM list of contents	*EM list of contents*
Grade 6	Welcome, friends A Fancy Dress Show A Seashore A Park A Village Fair In the School Compound What Time Is It now? The Environment Day (From Nataraj *et al.*, 1998: 3)	A Voyage to Lilliput Farewell to the Farm The Changing World Abraham Lincoln (Parts 1 and 2) Don Quixote Meets a Company of Actors The Poet's House Woodman, Spare That Tree! City streets and Country roads (From Jadeja *et al.*, 1999: 2)
Grade 8	(No authors provided) *Poetry*: (optional) Rhyme Rhyme Rhyme Only One Mother The Picnic Two Birds	*Poetry:* Under the Greenwood Tree (William Shakespeare) She Dwelt among the Untrodden ways (William Wordsworth) To a child dancing in the wind (W. B. Yeats) The Listeners (Walter de la Mare) Coming (Phillip Larkin) A blackbird singing (R.S.Thomas)
	Prose: Let's begin Hello! I am Vipul A Railway Station At the Zoo On the Farm Good Manners In the Kitchen (From Kotak *et al.*, 1999: 4)	*Prose:* Little Children Wiser than Men (Leo Tolstoy) Do You Know? (Clifford Parker) My Financial Career (Stephen Leacock) The Lady is an Engineer (Patricia Strauss) The Judgement Seat of Vikramaditya (Sister Nivedita) (From Thaker, 1999: 2)
Grade 10	*Poetry* (optional) Laughing Song (Blake) In the Night (Naidu) Wander Thirst (Gerald Gould) The Secret of the Machines (Rudyard Kipling)	*Poetry:* Blow, Blow, Thou Winter Wind (Shakespeare) London (Blake) Upon Westminster Bridge (Wordsworth) To – (Shelley) La Belle Dame Sans Merci (Keats) The Professor (Nissim Ezekeil) The Fountain (Lowell)
	Prose (no authors provided) An Act of Service Strange But True Have You Heard This One? Vaishali at the Police Station Prevention of Cruelty to Animals The Indian Village – Then and Now (From Kotak *et al.*, 1998)	*Prose:* Ramanujam (C.P. Snow) On Saying Please (A.G. Gardener) The Home Coming (Tagore) Andrew Carnegie (E. H. Carter) A Day's Wait (Hemmingway) After Twenty Years (O' Henry) Vikram Sarabhai (M.G.K. Menon) (From Vamdatta *et al.*, 2000: 44)

Lamb (grade 9), Vivekanand and Shelley (grade 10), Lord Byron (grade 11) and Kingsley Amis (grade 12). Also, all of the prose and poetry selections are 'original' literary pieces and are identified by the authors who wrote them. The comprehension/writing questions at the end of these readings emphasize the importance of interpreting, questioning and decoding authorial stances/intentions. The following are examples:

(1) How does E.M. Forster describe tolerance? How does Forster distinguish between love and tolerance? (Khan *et al.,* 2000: 74, based on E.M. Forster's essay, 'Tolerance')
(2) How does Churchill justify Britain's stand during the war? Do you agree with his views? (Moses *et al.,* 2000: 107, based on Churchill's essay, entitled 'Speech to Congress')
(3) Why, according to Joad, does money and power not make us civilized? Why do Shakespeare, Beethoven and Raphael matter for civilization? (Vamdatta *et al.,* 2000: 158, based on C.E.M. Joad's essay, entitled 'A Dialogue on Civilization')
(4) The poet, Keats, has asked several questions in this poem. Are they answered? What are your answers to these questions (Purani *et al.,* 1998: 127, based on a poem by John Keats entitled 'Song')

VM texts, in contrast, for grades 5–9 ask no such questions, leaving one with the impression that delving into authors' minds in order to capture authorial intentions in English is irrelevant for GM students. As mentioned previously, exercises at the end of readings in these texts are limited to explanations of and exercises for grammar points.

Discussion

Moving away from text-based specifics, I would like to move onto addressing the differences in the textbooks in terms of their relevance in broader educational contexts. Hornberger's (2000) bilingual continua reminds us that learners are positioned at different points of several co-existing planes of literacy development. In the present discussion of divergent cultural models, students schooled in the VM seem to have exposure to more 'relatively nativized' versions of Indian English than their EM counterparts and their literacies can, in many ways, be regarded as emergent literacies. A co-occurrence of several identifiable features in VM and EM texts partially allows us to see how the two sets of texts construct relatively separate 'detachable' literacy events that draw on divergent cultural models of English language literacy which ultimately produce very different *literate-in-English* candidates (Figure 3.2).

Table 3.2 Differences in English literacy cultural models for GM and EM students

Cultural models regarding English literacy for GM students	Cultural models regarding English literacy for EM students
• Survival English is adequate (English literacy being presented as discrete skills, focus on teaching the minutia of writing (capital letters, writing neatly on a line, punctuation) • Local knowledge is adequate (readings concentrate on small, local contexts); very few readings by international authors, few readings addressing global concerns • Assumption that teachers themselves are not fluent enough in English ('explanation' sections in texts addressed to both teachers and students in Gujarati and English) • Cannot learn by themselves/no need to enhance independent learning/thinking (no self-learning/composition sections)	• Developing English language skills to engage in complex reasoning about civic issues, social matters, developing a voice in their writing, having them engage in compositions/essays where their opinions count • More cosmopolitan: readings by American, British and Indian-English authors, issues with a more global slant • No such assumption in EM texts (no 'explanation' sections, instructions largely to students and only in English; tips for teachers on how to develop 'creative' assignments) • A premium on independent learning/building confidence, with 'self-learning' exercises

This somewhat simplistic breakdown allows one to see that 'literacy in English' means very different things for the two sets of students with English language textbooks being partially used as key instruments in perpetuating this divergence. Access to professional, tertiary-level institutions in India by VM students is seriously hampered because, among other things, these institutions are disproportionately oriented to privileging students schooled in the EM and – as it will be clearer in Chapters 4 and 5 – because Vernacular/Gujarati ways of writing, believing, thinking, reasoning and acting are not valued. At the college level, their general situation becomes more poignant when they are expected to compete with their EM counterparts, especially in English examinations in their final year of college. Not only are they contending with having learned only survival English, they are, by and large, also contending with not having access to the general *assumptions nexus* (explained earlier in Chapter 2) that middle-class Indians can claim with their 'mother's milk': exposure to cosmopolitan texts, to reading and writing about social/textual issues, to working independently and to voicing opinions. I distinctly remember my GM friends in college struggling with Dryden and Restoration poetry while EM students like me had a much easier time with it. Not only had we had extensive contact, practice and rehearsal with English poetry, it was part of our 'regular' curriculum that we took for granted: this was how 'things were supposed to be' (a cloak that fell off very quickly and very early in this endeavor). Thus, it would appear that it is the concomitant values, ideas, ways of thinking, being, reasoning, reading and writing that EM students have, acquire and, in some sense, 'assume' (since it is so naturalized and 'detachable') on which a large part of professional, tertiary-level instruction in India seems to build.

This area of what is 'assumed' and aligned with what in cultures begs to be uncovered (Ramanathan, 2002b). K–12 social and textbook-based practices are 'framed' by particular behaviors and motions that both sets of students bring with them and these are built on later at college level, thereby rendering them relatively aligned, 'detachable' cultural models. Recalling Wartenberg's point regarding alignment, even in situations in which we might characteristically describe one person as having power over another, that power depends upon other persons/institutions/groups acting in alignment with what the first person does. It is in this context that we can understand Foucault's assertion that power is everywhere, not because it embraces everything but because it comes from everywhere. In this sense, the textbooks under examination are visible cultural artifacts that are framed by other events to make them embedded in a complex web of power structures. As Foucault (1972, 1978) would argue, it is the heterogeneity of the alignments (*dispositifs*) that dispose power: they include not just agents but also the instruments of power (buildings, documents, tools, etc.) including, of course, textbooks (as in the present case) and the practices and rituals through which they are deployed (Cummins, 2000).

This, however, does not mean that power flows only one way. Canagarajah's (1999a) study shows how students in Shri Lanka resist English and the power they associate with it in small but significant ways (and indeed parts of the next two chapters will show how individual institutions and teachers work to resist and critically counter the English–Vernacular chasm). The present focus on how textbooks exert power is most selective in this regard: they constitute but one facet albeit a significant one in a larger, elaborate socio-educational system. But as Apple and Christian-Smith (1991) remind us:

[T]exts are not simply 'delivery systems' of 'facts.' They are at once the results of political, economic, and cultural activities, battles, and compromises. They are conceived, designed, and authored by real people with real interests. They are published within the political and economic constraints of markets, resources, and power. And what texts mean and how they are used are fought over by communities with distinctly different commitments and by teachers and students as well.

Because power circulates and is produced from one moment to the next, it does, over time and with re-enactment with aligned facets, sustain a power relationship (Rouse, 1994). The (de-voicing) role that English plays in this complex picture is not be undermined at all. The combination of perspectival metadiscourse, the westernized readings, the space for individual views and opinions, the comprehension exercises that ask students to probe and reason about civic and social issues along are partially based on a set of teaching and learning cultural models practices that prepare one kind of 'literate-in-English' person. However, the combination of informational metadiscourse, the focus on grammar and survival English and the lack of space for self-learning and essay writing and the general de-emphasis on developing 'critical reading' skills in English contribute to an alternate 'literate-in English' candidate, with the former winning out over the latter. Textbook representations of English literacy, then, are but surface manifestations that tell of deeply embedded differences between the 'educated' and the not, 'successful' and the not, 'sophisticated' and the not, 'westernized' and the not but they, like most things in the educational realm, need to be first recognized as 'legitimatized' grooves that demand probing. Colonial legacy and postcolonial practice: English falls centrally in this divide.

Notes

1. The English taught in VM textbooks is referred to as 'lower-level' English, while the English in EM textbooks is called 'higher-level' English. Terms that appear on the covers of the textbooks, they can be seen partially to indicate a 'legitimized' chasm between the two mediums.
2. The one point they seem to have in common is that they are all culturally embedded and are more or less obviously at work all the time, with particular facets of their nature being highlighted in certain contexts as opposed to others.
3. This set in motion a drastically different perception, since in the 18th century, India and Indian culture was merely regarded as alien, not inferior (Suleri, 1992).
4. I am using the term 'metadiscourse' in the way Crismore (1984) uses it to refer to authors 'discoursing about discourse'. Detailing the various levels at which metadiscourse can be seen to function, Crismore (1988) maintains that it can function at a referential, informational level, when it directs readers how to comprehend the primary message by referring, for instance, to its text structure or the author's discourse goals ('I will describe X'). It can also function at an expressive, attitudinal plane when it serves to direct readers towards understanding the author's perspective or stance toward the content of the primary message.
5. VM textbooks do not have such summaries: readings in these texts typically begin with a list of vocabulary items around particular topics, e.g. 'at the fair', 'at the post office', 'buying a train ticket').
6. The writing requirements for EM texts in contrast range from 'writing answers to questions based on the text' (grade 5) to 'writing and building stories on given points'(grade 6) to 'writing essays based on the text' (grade 7).

Chapter 4

The Divisive Politics of Divergent Pedagogical Practices at College Level

Mr. P. sits in his little office in the parking lot. He coordinates the National Social Service (a voluntary social service organization) from this little work place that holds two desks and a cupboard. Female students trickle in, giving him oral and written reports about their team projects in the rural villages outside Ahmedabad: on the number of polio vaccines they were able to administer to babies, on lessons in hygiene they taught some women, on bank accounts they were able to open for some women, on Gujarati lessons they were able to provide small children after schooling, on bus services they were able to coordinate for those students in the inner-city, who because of curfew imposed after the Hindu–Muslim riots, could not make it to the examination centres to take their final Board examinations. Mr. P. listens to them all, advises, comments, interjects, reassures. A bell clangs marking the end of his free period. He picks up his books, turns to me and says 'I am teaching Dryden's "The Rape of the Lock" today. Do you want to come? Come on, then… ' (Aavee cheh? Chalo to, jaiyeh)
(Field notes, July 2000)

By identifying and analysing K–12 English language textbooks, the previous chapter partially discussed ways in which VM and EM students placed as they are on divergent points of various literacy continua are socialized into unequal cultural models. It is these divergent cultural models that, among other things, the two sets of students bring to the college scene. Moving into addressing some local realities in two different colleges, this chapter offers glimpses into two divergent socio-educational worlds. The two institutions, representing two very different student populations, are a low-income VM college and an upper-middle-class private college. The lower-income institution is an all-women's college that offers a BA degree; the upper-middle-class college is a new private, co-educational college that offers a bachelor's degree in Business Administration. The key questions that haunt this chapter are as follows:

(1) Where and how is English instruction located in these two divergent institutions, and what role does medium of instruction seem to play in the respective contexts?
(2) How do teachers and students at both institutions mitigate the English–Vernacular gulf?

Addressing these issues will bring us closer to understanding how English is situated amidst other languages worldwide (Smith & Forman, 1997) and what this means for the social advancement of college-going students in Gujarat. It will also allow us to see the ways in which the current postcolonial combination of particular state-wide, institutional and classroom-specific educational practices work simultaneously to sustain the English–Vernacular gulf, while also producing pockets of specific resistance to bridge the chasm. While the chapter will call attention to the divergent worlds of EM and VM, it will also concentrate on how individual teachers, such as Mr P. in the excerpt heading this chapter, complicate the scene by working against perceived gulfs. Teachers like him, as we shall see, find ways of effecting change in the lives of their students and, thus, on the larger world 'peripheral' to the classroom. Likewise, students find subtle ways to make their resentment and animosity against the larger system from the periphery clear as well. As we will see later in the chapter, the 'peripheral' is crucial to what goes on in the classroom.[1]

As I mentioned in Chapter 1, splitting this chapter to address first gulfs and then bridges runs the risk of not addressing the overlapping, interwoven and fluid nature of the larger teaching/learning enterprise. Classrooms, pedagogic practices, teachers' beliefs, student attitudes, ideologies, institutionalized practices all impinge on a teaching/learning scene at once. My sense-making process and the discursive act of capturing some prominent features in these scenes renders the gulfs and bridges as separate when they are not. Mr P. is indeed, talking about and doing critical practice at the same time as he is hastening off to teach 18th-century British Literature to VM students. To him, organizing buses that will pick up VM female Muslim students from curfew-bound areas in downtown Ahmedabad is just as imperative as teaching Dryden in Gujarati. As with the earlier chapters, my voice moves unevenly from reporting, to interpreting, to analysing and interpreting again.

Positioning Myself: Being Native and Distanced, Being an Insider and Not — Issues of Methodology and Raw Materials

In Chapter 2, I detailed ways in which the Indian middle class has relatively unquestioning access to the assumptions nexus – a phrase that captures how and why things are the way they are and the importance of fighting the continuing entrenchment of the nexus. As noted in that chapter, this phrase partially explains the vast array of class-based social practices both inside and outside the home that privilege the middle class, and that, by their very existence, subordinate low-income groups. The term includes everything in class-related conventions that inform how and why particular class groups live and make the choices they do in almost every realm of everyday existence, including opting for EM education. Over time, this nexus, comprised partly of the general educational system and class-related assumptions, values and conventions, assumes 'naturalized' overtones. Identifying and exploring how some of the social cogs in the system – language policies and pedagogic practices in the present case – connect with each other to produce particular systematic consequences – allows us to see how power circulates through the 'system' and is distributed across a range of social networks.

The juxtaposition of the two institutions I present here is deliberate. I had initially begun this segment of the project by concentrating only on the women's college when I realized that as an EM middle-class researcher, I was bringing too many of my assumptions and values to the site. It became imperative, at that point, for me to find another diametrically opposed institutional context (in terms of gender, disciplinary focus and class) and the business college came closest to fitting that bill. It can be argued, of course, that by choosing to concentrate on two such different institutions I was, in effect, comparing apples and oranges and, while this may be true to some extent, I should assert that the overall point of the comparison was get a fuller sense of the general worlds of these two divergent sets of students and to locate and understand the divergent pedagogic practices in each. Exploring two institutions that fall toward either end of a class/privilege spectrum affords us insights into the gulf that stretches in between, thereby setting up a backdrop against which to understand how individual teachers work at mitigating the gulf.

To get a fuller sense of the divergences between the two schools, I attempted to visit both colleges every day. I would typically take a rickshaw down-town to the women's college in the late morning (the college began at 11:00) and would head to the business college in the afternoon (by about 2:30 or so). Going back and forth between the two colleges made some class-related aspects stand out sharply: the fact that the women's college was buried in a small side-street and had no campus grounds or cafeteria to speak of, and the business college was not, that the former was located in the thick of traffic, sounds of which impeded listening in the classroom and the latter was not; that the former was in a relatively 'unsafe' part of town given recent Hindu–Muslim riots, while the other was not: that several of the students at the women's college seemed relatively hesitant and unsure in their general demeanor in ways that female students at the business college did not. These were the glaring differences that I was constantly aware of as the rickshaw left the premises of one institution and took me to the other. The subtler differences – in classroom practices, student goals and teacher expectations – became obvious as I began my class observations and interviewing (see Appendix 1 for details).

I began by sitting in on the English language classes at both institutions (referred to as 'English Compulsory' at the women's college and 'Commercial English' at the business one). However, in order to get a fuller sense of how teaching in these classes compared to the teaching of other subjects at both institutions, I also observed a range of other classes, including Sanskrit, Statistics, Economics, Psychology, Gujarati, Hindi and Sociology at the former and Growth of Industries, Economics, Principles of Management, Business Organization and Accountancy at the latter (see Appendixes 1 and 4 for a break down of classes and a sample 'Commercial English' examination). I was, thus, able to contextualize, to some degree, the English language teaching and learning (ELTL) amidst other courses offered at both institutions. Observations included everything from documenting the number of students, their seating arrangements, recording their chatter, to making notes of what the teacher was saying and writing on the board, directives about assignments and the general framing of class activities.

I attempted to interview as many people as possible in both institutions. Interviewees included administrators, faculty members, students, representative clerks and the former dean of commerce at the university. At the women's college, I interviewed two administrators, eight faculty members and 25 students. These were typically conducted in Gujarati or Hindi and then translated into English while transcribing. At the business college I interviewed one administrator, five faculty members and thirty-two students. Interviews at this institution were almost entirely in English (see Appendix 1 for a partial list of interview themes).

It was difficult to get an equal number of written documents from both colleges; however, I was able to acquire some overall general information regarding course and examination policies and English-language textbooks for both institutions. Because colleges in the city are part of a larger, centralized university system, they have to follow university-mandated syllabi and curricular rules and written information regarding these was available at both colleges. But local, institution-specific documentation was not nearly as easy to get, especially from the women's college. Because of the paucity of its resources, this institution does not put out any printed documentation to speak of (*'Paper ghanu mehengu chhe'* [paper is very expensive]). All notices here are handwritten on blackboards, including information about 12th-grade scores, upcoming social events and course timetables. Notices regarding courses are handwritten by faculty members on blackboards in respective classrooms: handouts are conspicuously absent. The business college, in contrast, has glossy, detailed brochures advertising several programmes; printed notices are evident on bulletin boards; and teachers bring photocopied handouts to class.

All of these raw materials were systematically combed and coded for themes, a number of which emerged in varying forms in the different kinds of data collected in the two institutions. The recurring themes form the crux of this chapter, and the various subsections – especially those relating to pedagogic practices and the socio-cultural assumptions feeding them – partially illustrate what these themes are. Both horizontal and vertical dimensions of the data were carefully juxtaposed against each other and analysed. The horizontal (or historical dimension) 'refers to description of events and behaviors as they evolve over time...the vertical dimension refers to factors which influence behaviors and interactions at the time at which they occur' (Nunan, 1992: 58). As the chapter reveals, I attempted to get at both historical factors that have shaped the orientations of the two colleges and the current, local factors that are being negotiated even as this book is written and read.

Gujarat-specific Language Policies

At least two state-wide language policies impact on the institutional realities explored in this chapter and I would like, in this section, to address them. They are: (1) free education for females, from K–12 and beyond (for both EM and VM students) and (2) state-wide examinations and 'external' assessment.

Free education for females

This was a policy that came about in the early to mid 1970s when the ruling political party in the state decided that making education free for females would both help one of the more underprivileged sectors of society and be a good political move that 'would garner the votes of the masses' (FI, 1: 1). This policy mandated that the only fees female students would be required to pay would be for examination paper, a payment that amounts to a fraction of what their male counterparts have to pay. (I do not believe I paid any fees all through my schooling, including for my BA and MA degrees). Also, in poorer colleges, textbooks for females are almost free as well. Such policies have allowed many more low-income women to obtain college degrees. However, because of a range of factors, including the 'peripheral' ones considered in this chapter, it is the middle-class, EM (female) students (enrolled in public institutions) that, by and large, reap the benefits of the system. As mentioned previously, not only do EM students have access to EM colleges and 'higher-level' disciplines – doors that largely remain shut for VM students – the socio-cultural worlds EM students such as myself operate in seem to dovetail with the society's social goods in ways that they do not for VM students.

State-wide examinations and external assessment

There are several state-wide examinations built into the educational system: at the K–12 level, students take common 'Board' examinations – examinations scheduled, administered and graded by the State Board of Education – at the 10th and 12th grades. (Tenth grade scores determine whether students are eligible for the arts, commerce or science streams, with the science stream demanding higher scores.) The 12th-grade scores, along with the years of English instruction they have had in school,[2] determine both the types of colleges to which they can apply and the disciplines in which they can major. At the college level, all students have to take state Board examinations at the end of each year, which are set, administered and graded by external examiners affiliated to the central university. The scores at the end of the final year of college partially determine admission[3] to, among other things, a postgraduate programme of study. These 'Board' examinations are graded by 'external examiners', a practice that was consistently deplored by all of the people interviewed at both institutions (indeed, naïve as I was then, I was one such disgruntled student who was convinced that my missing my first-class by a fraction in my BA was because my papers had been graded by a VM teacher!). Several complained about the university not maintaining high enough standards, about the English proficiency of the graders themselves, about the general veracity of the results and about how their best students get down-graded (and miss their 'first-classes' or 'distinctions'). Several faculty members felt that all they could do was to teach their students the best way they knew how and 'then hope for the best, since there is no saying with the examination system here' (FL, 2: 8, a theme I grew up hearing). It is against this partial background that the individual efforts by teachers trying to counter the system (Simon, 1992) need to be understood and validated.

Describing the Institutions: Two Divergent Campuses and Student Populations

The women's college (WC)

Located in downtown Ahmedabad, the women's college (WC) emerges amidst snarling traffic and thick crowds. There are no campus grounds to speak of, just a tall three-storey building that one enters through a parking lot filled with scooters and bicycles. Thepremises offer two degrees: it serves as a liberal arts college for women from 11:00a.m.–4:45p.m. and it is a co-educational law college from 5p.m. til 10p.m. Established some years before Gujarat adopted its policy regarding free literacy for women, the WC began 34 years ago with the primary purpose of providing a 'safe environment for young women to study' (FI, 2: 2). Its hours have been deliberately set from late morning to early evening to meet local, class-related, cultural demands on women: 'these young women have to finish all their jobs at home' (including the cooking, gathering water in buckets and pots in the mornings since water in the inner city is available only from 7–9a.m. and caring for the infirm/elderly members of the household, e.g. grandparents).

Almost all of the women in the college are from VM backgrounds and almost all of them speak Gujarati as their first language at home. Most of them have scored poorly in the 12th-grade examinations and have settled on this college because it is one of the few colleges in the city that will admit them. Several students – especially those commuting from rural areas outside the city – mentioned choosing the college because it was conveniently located near a central bus station in the city, thus alleviating commuting problems. Many of the Muslim students that attend this college live in parts of downtown Ahmedabad that has seen gory violence with the recent outbreaks of Hindu–Muslim riots. Most of these students are very vocal about the role of the conservative BJP (Baharatiya Janata Party) Hindu government in fanning ethnic tensions. For some, the college is a haven: as one of the Muslim students puts it, 'I have my friends here; I know if violence breaks out, my professors here will keep me safe' [*Mere sab friends yahin hain; hadthaal hoga tho yahaan ke sab teachers mujhe safe rakhenge*] (SI, 19: 7). Still others said they opted for this institution because of its 'all girls' (SI, 1: 4) policy: their parents did not want them in classes where there were young men, since proximity with the opposite sex 'would not be alright' [*tthik nahi rahega*] (SI, 20: 1).

The young women do not really have places to sit in the parking lot and make do with the limited options available to them: on scooters or on the steps leading up to the class rooms before and between classes, chatting idly, consulting each other's class notes or eating roasted peanuts from a vendor who has parked his basket in the parking lot. The clothes of the young women, among other things, index their class background. All of the young women are traditionally dressed in *salwar-kameez* outfits (loose pants with a loose, long top and a scarf) with long, oiled and braided hair. Some of the better-off women wear heeled shoes: the rest are in sandals and rubber flip-flops. Almost all of them are deferential when speaking with male professors in hallways, during or after class or in the common faculty room. It was a common sight for several of them to linger outside the faculty room trying to summon up the courage to speak to a male teacher and, when they did so, their manner was tentative. Most of the teachers in the college are middle-class people who have themselves, for the most part, been schooled in Gujarati. Some of them have taught at the K–12 level before coming to this institution and claim familiarity with pedagogic practices into which their students may have been socialized. Many do not hesitate to draw on and extend these practices in their classes at the WC.

The college admits about 800 to 1000 students each year and the average class size is about 125 students. The institution follows the curriculum laid out by the centralized university to which it is affiliated.[4] All of the teaching – including English literature – is done in Gujarati. As the chair of the English department says: 'One of the prerequisites for teaching English literature here [in the WC] is that the candidate knows Gujarati fluently; whether he/she knows English is secondary. The teacher has to be able to communicate with the students in Gujarati' (FI, 1: 2). All English department faculty at the WC concurred with this view in my interviews with them.

The private business college (BC)

Located in the 'better' part of town, the business college (BC) is not nearly as engulfed by traffic as the WC is. Set amidst trees, the institution itself is removed from the street and, for the most part, secluded from street noise. This institution seems to have everything that the WC did not: quiet, space, a canteen for students to hang out in, a well-stocked library, drinking fountains. Groups of students mill at the entrance of the driveway, several stand in groups at tea stalls sipping tea, some sit on benches under trees. At this co-educational college, the students seem to tote clear markings of an upper-middle-class culture: a high degree of westernization (evidenced partly in the extensive amount of English spoken among teachers and students), relatively easy interaction between the sexes, the clothes (with all the young men in jeans and the young women in an even mix of jeans, and skirts, and Indian outfits), the generally un-oiled hair and the comparatively fancy shoes (no rubber flip-flops here).

The school offers various commerce degrees,[5] although it is the more recently implemented bachelor's degree in Business Administration (BBA) that this chapter draws on. College hours like those of the WC are from 11:00a.m. till 5p.m. The BBA degree is a three-year degree to which students gain admission after their 12th-grade examinations.[6] The average tuition fees for students who want to gain admission by 'buying seats' (because their 12th-grade scores were not high enough) is between Rs15,000–25,000 ($350–550) while the tuition for those who get in on merit is about Rs7000 ($155). About 75% of the students who enroll for this degree are from business homes, with many of them planning to join family-owned businesses or expand existing ones. The college typically admits about 120 students each year (there are a total of 350–375 students enrolled in all three years of college), who get divided into two sections of 60 students each. All instruction is in English only. All of the teachers know Gujarati and Hindi but few resort to using it in the classroom,[7] careful to follow institutional mandates about using only English in this EM setting. All teacher–student interactions seem relatively easygoing. Students do not seem to hesitate to approach their instructors outside class and to ask questions during a lesson.

Pedagogic Practices, Procedural Display, Social Conventions

I address two key points in this section: (1) the use of divergent pedagogic practices in the two institutions and (2) uncovering latent, 'peripheral' socio-cultural assumptions (of students and teachers) that partially inform the pedagogic practices. While there are definite similarities in pedagogic practices in the two institutions, there are marked differences as well, primarily relating to the differences in the medium of instruction. Aspects of classroom practices in the two institutions demonstrate features of *procedural display* (Bloome *et al.*, 1989) between teachers and students. Bloome *et al.* (1989: 272) compare procedural display to

a group of actors who have memorized their roles and who enact a play for each other's benefit without necessarily knowing what happens in the play or what the play means. Teachers and students may enact a lesson, say what 'needs' to be said to each other, move through and complete the lesson, without necessarily knowing or engaging in academic content; yet, they are constructing an event called a lesson that has cultural significance. *Simply put, procedural display occurs when teachers and students are displaying to each other that they are getting the lesson done, constructing a cultural event within a cultural institution – which is not at all the same thing as substantive engagement in some academic content.* (My emphasis)

This playing out of parts, as we shall presently see – with teachers teaching and students 'studenting' – although an integral part of formal schooling behavior is worked out in different ways in the present case.

Procedural display at the WC: Integrating the vernacular

Pedagogic practice 1: Drawing on Vernacular traditions in language class-rooms

One consistently recurrent feature in all the classes observed at the WC is the use of particular prosodic cues by teachers that serve to elicit choral responses from students (Goodwin, 2001). Some teachers, in the middle of their lectures, would ask questions and statements that seemed to orient students' choral utterances in distinct, chant-like ways. I first made these observations in the English and Sanskrit literature and language classes but found versions of them in other classes as well, although they were not nearly as frequently used in content-area classes as they were in the language classes. (These were practices I was not generally familiar with, except in Sanskrit classes when each class typically began with a choral recitation of assigned Sanskrit mantras.) The following excerpts taken from classes of Sanskrit, English, economics and psychology are representative examples of this kind of interaction. All of the classes were second-year (SY) classes. Examples 1 and 2 are from a Sanskrit class, 3 and 4 are from an opening class in English, while 4 and 5 are from economics and psychology respectively. Interactions in all classes were in Gujarati. I have highlighted the English words borrowed into the ongoing Gujarati class interactions.

Sanskrit class

Example 1 (from the Sanskrit class)

1   **T:**   *kaya **text** laavanu cche?* [Which text is to be bought?]
2   **Sts:** [responding chorally] *Kaadambari text laavanu cche.* [Kadambari (a
3   Sanskrit play) is to be bought.]
4   **T:**   *kyan thhi laavanu cche?* [Where is it to be bought from?]
5   **Sts:** *Ratan pol maathi laavaanu cche.* [From Ratan pol.]

Example 2 (from the Sanskrit class)

1   **T:**   *tho eh vakhate Avanti eh, kone?* [So at that time Avanti, who?]
2   **Sts:** *Avanti.*
3   **T:**   *Avanti eh kharraab laagyu. Su laagyu?* [Avanti felt bad. What did she
          feel?]

4   Sts: [responding chorally] *Kharraab laagyu.* [Felt bad.]

Example 3 (from the Sanskrit class)

1   T: *Kayaa form karvaana chhe ame?* [What form are we doing this
            year?]
2   Sts: *comedy form* [said in English].
3   T: *Ane kaaya **playwright** vaanchvaanu chhe?* [And which playwright
            are we reading?]
4   Sts: **Wilde**

Example 4 (from the English class)

1   T: *Tho, **Millie** eh light joyu. Suu joyuu?* [Millie saw a light. What did
            she see?]
2   Sts: **Light** *joyuu.* [Saw a light.]

Example 5 (from an economics class)

1   T: **GNP** *etle shuu?* [What does GNP mean?]
2   Sts: **Gross national product** [said in English].

Example 6 (from a psychology class)

1   T: *aah kone kahyuu?* [Who said this?]
2   Sts: **Skinner** *eh kayuu.* [Skinner said this.]

In each of these excerpts, the questions on the part of the teacher are
uttered in distinct ways: slowly in a sing-song manner with an exaggerated
rise at the end.[8] Teachers frequently seem to move into this mode of eliciting student participation during class. General explanations given by the
language teachers for using this method so extensively ranged from 'clas-
sical languages like Sanskrit have always been sung or chanted; singing
and chanting allows you to memorize information' (FI, 5: 42) to 'this is what
they have been used to in school and other non-schooling areas' (FI, 8: 41).
Indeed, as some instructors and students pointed out, this kind of elicita-
tion of choral responses was not unusual, especially in temples during
'*kathas*' (or discourses) where priests take myths and explain their relevance
to everyday living *(ameh katha maa kevi rithe kahiye cche?* [How do we speak
in Kathas?]), an explanation that resonated with my own experiences
where I, as a child, attended *Kathas* on key Hindu festivals. There is, then, a
seamless transference of valued community practices into classroom
realms, a transference that at once validates both the community practice
and what students bring with them to the classroom setting. Breaking off to
ask the questions that prompt these responses serves the dual purpose of

ensuring audience participation as well as serving as a viable way to test attention. One of the instructors who also gives these *Kathas* in local temples (indeed, many of the students had attended these sessions) maintained that chorusing responses – a marker of a strong oral, Vernacular tradition (Crook, 1996) – allows novices to engage in learning without apprehension of being judged. Several of the interviewed students said they often picked up 'answers' from their friends in such responses and that they could recognize the intonational cues of their teachers' voices that prompted such responses because they were used to it in other relatively less non-academic and non-institutionalized settings. When transferred to the realm of language teaching, all of the faculty members at this institution maintained that choral recitations and chants aided learning. As one Gujarati instructor explains: 'I use it to get participation, and then I go on' (FI, 4: 1). Drawing on the Vernacular, both as a medium and for purposes of relating to content, is also iterated in the instruction given to K–12 teachers in one of their teacher-education textbooks. The following excerpt from one such text discusses when teachers can draw on the mother tongue when teaching:

- The teacher may use the mother tongue to explain the peculiarity of certain sounds in English and to compare them with sounds in the mother tongue.
- He may use the mother tongue to explain unfamiliar words when the explanation of those words in English is more difficult than the words themselves, e.g. abstract nouns, ideas, etc.
- He may use the mother tongue to explain abstract words, phrases, and idioms.
- He may explain some particular grammatical points of the English language in the mother tongue to make those points easy for the pupils to learn. At times the teacher may compare and contrast the grammatical points in English and in the mother tongue.
- He may use the mother tongue to help pupils to collect ideas and then to organize them when they prepare to write compositions.
- He may use the mother tongue to teach pupils different types of reading.
- He may use the mother tongue in the classroom to test pupils' comprehension.
- He may use the mother tongue to help pupils to learn to use the dictionary.
- He may use the mother tongue when giving instructions to pupils. (Raval & Nakum, 1996: 103–4)

Several of the teachers at this college recall their respective VM schooling practices where the Vernacular was both heavily used and regarded as valuable and integral to language teaching. Indeed, as some of the teachers pointed out, not drawing on the Vernacular practices in the classroom seems unnatural ('some of these students may be poorer than me, but like them I grew up learning in this way, both in the classroom and outside it, especially in temples' [FI, 18: 5]).

Pedagogic practice 2: Collisions between medium and content

While the previous section discussed how teachers successfully draw on the Vernacular to elicit student participation, not all instances of Vernacular use work well. In the area of literature teaching, the English–Vernacular chasm seems particularly sharp, a point that has been made previously (Jawaare, 1998; Loomba, 1998; Tharu, 1997). This collision – between literature and language teaching – plays out in interesting ways in the WC. English literature in the WC is taught, by and large, in Gujarati, with occasional phrases in English. While drawing on the Vernacular to aid language/literature teaching is not new (Canagarajah, 1999b; Ramanathan, 2002b, 2003), the local consequences of it, in this particular case, are poignant because the (VM) students majoring in English have to take the state-board university examinations in English. Many of them really value the use of the Vernacular in teaching since it aids comprehension ('Otherwise I won't understand' [*nahin tho samjan naa aveh*] [SI, 39: 4]) but some also voice concern that the almost constant use of the Vernacular, while valuable in the classroom, handicaps their performance in year-end examinations when they have to compete with their EM counterparts taking the same examination.

Of the 25 students interviewed at the WC, all 16 English-major students felt that they found the content of what they were reading and learning about distant from their everyday existence, since most of the texts they contend with are western, literary texts ('Sometimes I wonder: "Do people over there [the west] speak like this? Think like this?" ' [*kabhi aisa lagtha hai vahaan ke log aise baat karte hain? aise sochte hain'?*]; 'Sometimes I don't understand their customs' [*kabhi kabhi unke rivaaz samaj hi nahi aata*]). The second-year 'English special' class (for students majoring in English) that I observed fairly consistently is a case in point. A required text for the class is *The Importance of Being Earnest* and the syllabus requires that students know both theories of comedy as a form and the text itself. In each of the observed classes, the teacher primarily used Gujarati to teach and, in instances when he lapsed into English, he typically followed it up with a direct translation in Gujarati ('How did drama begin?' [*Drama na udhbhog kevi rithe sharu thayu?*]). While reading the play aloud in English, the teacher laboriously translated each sentence, so that the larger comic scene seldom emerged. Students seemed to concentrate hard on figuring out the literal meaning of each sentence. Thus, while the teacher seemed to enjoy some of the comic scenes, laughing uproariously at moments, most of the students looked on uncomprehendingly. When the teacher tried to explain some of the comic elements in Gujarati, several of the students said that they could not see what was so funny. In one instance, the instructor spent about 15 minutes explaining sarcasm, a rhetorical turn that these students seemed unfamiliar with but one that was crucial to some of the humor in the scene they were collectively reading. When asked about it in a group interview, five of the students maintained that although they realized they needed the explanation on sarcasm, they did not find anything funny in what they were reading.

The poignancy of moments such as these, the general alienation that these students experience is caused by several competing factors, all tied to the English–Vernacular gulf: the content is culturally alien and far removed, the language in which the play is written is one they are not familiar with and the language in which the content is explained reduces a really funny scene to dullness and tedium, with traces of humor completely erased. The conflict between mediums – English in the text and the Vernacular in class – among other things does not help them gain fluency over either the language or the content/culture of what they are reading.

Pedagogic practice 3: Emphasizing 'correct answers'

The third pedagogic practice (at the WC) that stands out across classes – but in particularly exaggerated ways in the English classes – is the relative emphasis teachers place on 'correct answers'. All eight faculty members interviewed maintain that dictating 'questions and answers' and having students memorize them was a common pedagogic practice that they encouraged. Some of these 'correct answers' are from study guides (publications with ready-made questions and answers), others are from notes written by students in previous years and still others are notes taken in classes. Simplicity is one reason for emphasizing only one way of addressing a question: 'Keep it simple; no need for complications'. Other explanations ranged from 'See, these students have learned everything in Gujarati; giving them the question and the answer eases their burden' to 'We are asking these students to do what they are not used to, so we don't expect it of them here', to 'English remains foreign to them, time gets wasted' [*time waste thaaye cche*] (FI, 4: 2). For others, the emphasis on correct answers is related to the previously discussed point regarding choral responses, where questions are seen to have particular answers *(ameh jyaare prashna ek tareekeh puchiyeh, tho jawaab evi rithej aapvaanu'* [See asking questions in a certain way tells students that they have to respond in a certain way] [FI, 13: 2]). This emphasis on particular answers was evident in other contexts as well. Indeed, my classroom observations revealed that the questions students asked in class were restricted to requests to the teacher to repeat a point or to provide a 'correct answer'. When asked about it in group interviews, all of the students voiced discomfort not just at asking questions of their instructor ('How do I ask him?' [*Unko kaise poonche?*] [SI, 6: 3]) and at speaking English in front of their instructor but at feeling that they 'could scarcely figure out what the English text is saying, let alone ask questions about it' [*text hi samaj nahi aata, tho questions kahaan se pucche?*] (SI, 3: 4).

In summing up this section, then, several issues related to the English–Vernacular enterprise arise: the use and justification of choral recitation as pedagogic practices, the cultural dissonance between the content of the textbook and the medium (and cultural context) in which it is taught, along with the pedagogic practice of providing and eliciting 'correct answers' to specific, pre-planned questions cumulatively seem to inform procedural display at the WC. The general ELTL scenario at this institution, then, is complex, with some of the complexity extending into practices relating to oral, Vernacular traditions that students bring with them and that teachers draw on to facilitate teaching and learning, to others that relate to simplifying material as a way of mitigating perceived learning difficulties. All of these classroom issues are in varying ways related to the English–Vernacular gulf, a chasm which, as we shall see, is not really as wide at the BC.

Procedural display at the business college

Pedagogic practice 1: Group work and active participation
The collision between media of instruction is not nearly as apparent in the business college (BC) as in the WC. While there are some VM students here, their general English proficiency is relatively high. Students frequently raise hands to ask questions in class, many volunteer responses to queries and the lessons typically engage students in in-depth critical questioning of issues in texts.

A case in point is the following description of a class in business organization. This was a first-year (FY) class with 60 students. The class began with the instructor splitting the class into groups of five or six and assigning them to work on one of four business cases written up on a handout. Each of the four cases described a company or industrial unit failing because of one or several reasons. The students were to identify the reasons for failure based on the following criteria:

- lack of planning,
- lack of organizing including staffing, personnel issues,
- lack of direction – supervision, motivation, coordinating units or
- lack of control – feedback, reporting back to managers.

The groups break out into chatter for about 20 minutes, discussing the intricacies of the case assigned to them. Each group decides on its spokesperson who then goes to the front of the class and presents the group's collective analysis. Each of the spokespeople present their responses confidently and in detail, careful to point out areas that their response did not address and caveats in their reasoning because of insufficient information available about the case in question. While the English-speaking skills of the GM students was limited, they seem to struggle on confidently, seemingly unworried about grammatical mistakes. The class ends with students still talking about their group's responses in the hallways.

Although not all the classes at this college encourage group work – indeed, several had traditional lecture formats – they all seem to focus on working with texts and business cases, with a general de-emphasis on finding the 'correct answers'. Overall, the justification for this was given in business terms: 'Each business problem is different and each manager is going to handle the problem differently. So there cannot be correct answers, only appropriate ways of thinking through problems' (FI, 21: 3).[9] In terms of class participation, students in this context seemed comfortable asking content-based questions.

Focus on grammar in a business context

This level of heightened interaction seems evident in the English classes at this college as well. The English classes here (called Modern Commercial Communication) are oriented exclusively to business English and a significant portion of each class lesson was devoted to addressing aspects of grammar and word choice necessary for effective business communication. Indeed, the first chapter of the textbook for the first year brings up word-choice and grammar-related issues in the context of business letters. The following is an excerpt from a section entitled 'Correctness':

Language: If the language of a business letter is incorrect it creates a very bad impression about its writer. The reader might distrust the businessman who cannot write correctly. Rules of grammar must be followed. Care must be taken in small matters like spelling words. For example, the manufacturer does not *taste* saris before sending them to the market; he *tests* them. Similarly, words used in a letter must be appropriate. (Desai & Patel, 1999: 64)

Likewise, issues related to verbs get explained in a section entitled 'Forcefulness'. The following is an excerpt:

Besides, correctness, clarity, conciseness, courtesy and proper tone, there is one more important quality in a good business letter. The communication should be forceful… Active verbs should be used instead of passive verbs:

- The production of rice was higher in India during this year.
- India produced more rice during this year.
- There was no effect on the budget on prices.
- The budget did not affect prices.
- A revision of the policy is not necessary.
- There is no need to revise the policy. (Desai & Patel, 1999: 71–2)

That much of English and Vernacular language learning in India (when taught as second/foreign languages) tends to be oriented around grammar and translation methods has been previously discussed (Ramanathan, 1999). Although English instructors at both the WC and the BC and believe that grammar is what the students need in their English classes ('They need to know the basics' [FI, 7: 1]), the grammar lessons at the BC tend to be presented in business contexts: grammatical issues are addressed in terms of their relative importance to genres in business, including letters, memos and reports. VM students in this institution seem to find greater value in the English-language classes, since many felt that their 'grammar is still no good' (SI, 3); EM students, in contrast, while they found the grammatical issues 'boring', found value in the connections the instructor and the textbook made between grammar and the business world.

Pedagogic practices, thus, at the BC, reflect, to some extent, ways in which English and Vernacular teaching traditions are somewhat independent of each other. Indeed, none of the teachers brought up Vernacular practices as effective ways of teaching. Teachers at this college are, like the teachers at the WC, building on the cultural models that their students bring with them. In the WC, the cultural models are more oriented to the Vernacular; in the BC, the cultural models seem to be more oriented to westernized pedagogic practices. One way of gaining a more comprehensive understanding of the differences in classroom practices is by exploring the 'periphery' – in this case aspects of the larger socio-cultural worlds – the two contrasting student populations come from. The following section addresses some of these issues.

The 'Peripheral' at Both Colleges

I turn now to addressing some socio-cultural assumptions that feed into the divergent pedagogic practices detailed earlier. While these may seem 'peripheral', since they are after all 'outside' the classroom, they are crucial to address, since, as Holliday (1994: 31) points out, 'much of what we see happening in classrooms are "epiphenomena" – mere surface manifestations of far more complex things going on under the surface'. Indeed, as the following section points out, one can make strong connections between the classrooms and the worldviews held by teachers and students.

The socio-cultural worlds that the students at both colleges inhabit seem to be in stark contrast with each other. Interviews with students at the WC reveal some of the class-related and familial pressures they experience. Of the 25 students interviewed, 19 of them said that they ended up in the WC because this was the only college that would admit them (given their low 12th-grade score), while six said they chose it because of its convenient location ('I need to take only one bus to get here, if I chose a college in that side of town, I would need to take three buses' [*ek hi bus lena padtha hai; nahi to mujhe theen bus lena padega*] [SI,4: 3]. When asked about their plans after college, 22 of the 25 said that it would depend on their parents' wishes: 17 of these students also said that their parents had 'already begun looking' for an eligible match and that they would get married if everything was set up ('How can I say no; what my parents say I have to do' [*naa kaisa bole? Jo maa-baap bolenge, mujhe karna hi padega*]).[10] When asked about their personal desires all of them said they wanted to take computer classes after they had improved their English (since all computer-related materials, classes, jobs demand English fluency), five mentioned postgraduate degrees and the remaining 20 seemed undecided. All of them want jobs but say that good jobs demand fluency in English. Besides, it will all depend on the 'family they get married into; if they'll let me work, that'll be good' [*Job karne denge, tho ttik...*] (SI, 2: 1).

Some of the teachers at the WC are clearly sympathetic towards the predicaments of their students while others are not. Their comments range from 'these are low-caliber students' (FI, 8: 1) to 'They [the students] have a lot of pressure [to get married] and work at home' to 'They are in college only to pass time' [*Gher maa bhahuuj pressure cche; timepass maatej cche ahiyaan*] (FI, 6: 1). Several of the faculty attribute what they regard as 'low motivation' on the part of their students to familial pressure to get married. Several of them mentioned intervening and talking to parents in instances when the young women are not allowed to finish their final-year college examinations. 'I tell them "let her at least finish the degree"; sometimes they listen, sometimes they don't' (FI, 3: 3). Some of these same teachers are the ones that resist categorizing these students as 'low caliber' ('How can we say that of them? Look how far they have come with what they began?' [FI, 14: 2]).

Teachers and students bring very different teaching and learning assumptions to their classroom interactions at the BC. All of the faculty members maintained that they realized that the general motivation and aptitude of their students was relatively high, although most of the faculty did not have divergent teaching experiences with which to compare their current teaching experiences.[11] The one instructor who had taught at a college similar to the WC before his current job felt that the high levels of motivation in students at the business school were directly related to class ('The higher the class, the higher the enthusiasm… they have been to better schools and are familiar with the sorts of things we do in classes here. A lot of the students from municipality [Vernacular] schools say "we have never seen this type of teaching"' [FI, 8: 2]). The typical business background of the students seems to be another reason that teachers give for high motivation ('They opt for this degree because they are surrounded by aspects of it at home…they see their family members involved in it' [FI, 4: 3]). In student interviews, all 32 students felt that they would go on for higher study because 'just a BBA won't get you a good job' (SI, 4: 1). Regarding the women students in their classes, three of the five teachers maintained that the females in their classes are more outspoken than the young men with clear career goals ('All of the young women interviewed last week for a personality contest said they wanted to be business managers. Now whether they were saying that because we [faculty] were the judges [and that is what we wanted to hear] or whether they mean that, we don't know. From the girls in my class, I would say they mean it…' [FI, 8: 3]). None of the women (15 of the 32 students interviewed) seem to feel the sorts of pressures that their counterparts in the WC do. Of the 15 women, 12 said they were going on for MBA degrees after they receive their college degree. All of them maintained that their parents were the ones encouraging them to work hard in school ('Even when I want to do something in the house, my mother will tell me not to waste time doing it…to study only…That is what she keeps saying…' [SI, 18: 3]).

Struggles and Pressures of GM and EM Students at the BC

The divergent socio-cultural worlds described in previous sections are not intended to imply that tertiary-level education is rosy and smooth-sailing for all students at the BC. Both VM and EM students at this institution have their local struggles as well. Of the 32 students interviewed at this college, 10 had completed their K–12 in Gujarati. All of these students maintained that they were under pressure from home to get a degree from an EM college ('It's my parents' wish; if I get this degree in English-medium, then my life will be set' [*Mere ma-baap ka iccha hai...English-medium mein paddai hogi aur mera life set ho jaaye gaa...]* [SI, 5: 3]). All of these students struggle with keeping pace with the English used in theory-driven classes such as 'Growth of Industries', which offers a historical look at the development of small- and large-scale industrial units ('I have to keep my dictionary with me' [*Maaru dictionary saathej raakhu choon]'* [SI, 6: 1]). Of the 10, six are enroled in expensive English-language classes in the city, which they feel they have to do if they want to remain competitive with their EM counterparts. None of the 10 students felt that their English language classes in school prepared them to deal with English at the tertiary level ('Eight years I studied it and what's at the end of it? I can't even speak English' [*aant saal ke liye kiya, aur uske anth mein kya? Baath bhi nahi kar sakte English mein]* [SI, 3: 2]).

The EM students, however, have their own set of grievances too, the central of which had to do with university-level assessment procedures. All 22 of them unequivocally maintained that the graders hired by the university (all qualified lecturers teaching in different affiliated colleges) to grade the year-end examinations are largely VM instructors whose command over English is limited and who downgrade EM students because 'they don't understand what we write; they don't know enough English, so how can they grade well?' (SI, 3: 2). Indeed, all the instructors at both colleges lamented the assessment procedures at the university, which they collectively felt did not accurately reflect the performance of their students (several complained about corruption, leaked examination questions and poor enforcing of grading criteria among graders). At the BC, several instructors said that they worried about their EM students being disadvantaged ('The assessment process in our system has basically failed our students. They're really good students and they end up with low percentages at these examinations which lowers their chances in other competitive areas [higher education, jobs]' [FI, 3: 3]).

Bridging the English–Vernacular Chasm: Local Attempts at Critical Practice

This section shifts directions by directly exploring ways in which individual teachers and clusters of students work to mitigate the English–Vernacular gulf. Both colleges have instructors that work to reach out to VM students and do so in ways that are in keeping with the institutional realities of which they are a part. In the WC, these efforts seem more indirect than at the business institution, with some of the faculty realizing that they need first to boost their students' confidence levels in non-academic arenas as a way of partially addressing student problems of low motivation in general. As one instructor puts it, 'Teaching them English is not going to do it; that has to come later, if they want it'. Toward incorporating crucial, non-academic confidence-building measures into the college, one instructor began a local chapter of the National Social Service (NSS) at the WC.[12] This is a nation-wide volunteer organization that trains students in the rudimentaries of social work and sends them out in teams to work (primarily poor, rural, villages and farms) on special projects that range from inoculating babies in villages, to raising awareness about health issues, to doing investigations on the purity of water in particular regions. While none of these projects is directly related to English or Vernacular teaching, they are crucial to the empowering and confidence-building measures undertaken by the school. Recalling the pro-Vernacular sentiments of the Remove English Lobby (REL, detailed in Chapter 2), these measures are often couched in terms of 'strengthening one's [Vernacular] roots' (FI, 5: 2) and 'awakening in students the spirit of self-reliance' (FI, 14: 3). As the primary coordinator of the social service teams puts it:

> Having them engaged in an extra-curricular project such as this makes them really strong citizens. They are learning to take pride in so many different things at the same time: their background, their home language, their communities. These students have a lot of [low] self-confidence issues. Most of them want to be like you: they would have liked to have gone to EM schools and done well. Now they are beginning to see that being in the VM is really valuable: many of them will not be able to do the community work if they did not know Gujarati. You, for instance, would not be able to do what many of them are doing. Some of them have even told me they are not as crazy about English anymore. Suddenly they are realizing that they can be self-reliant with their mother tongue. (FI, 14: 5)

While this teacher did not explicitly mention the REL in his remarks to me, connections to this thought collective are resonant (Ramanathan, 2002a), especially in relation to 'being awakened' to value their home languages. The following excerpt from the lobby's formal treatise, translated from the original Hindi, shows how closely the teachers' views dovetail with the grassroots activism of the REL:

> The *Angrezi Hataao* movement is not like any other average movements.

This not a national party, it is a movement...It does not aim to achieve any goals, but aims to *awaken the public*...The organizers of the movement hope that each small movement that emanates from this one will operate on its own and will not depend wholly on the central organization...This work has to start this year itself and what better time for it, since this is the year of Gandhiji's anniversary? ...

The public should be made clear that this movement is not the vehicle of any particular national party, but is a movement that aims to reawaken the national spirit so as to allow us to recognize ourselves through our local cultures and heritages (*The New World*, 8 October 1968; my emphasis).

The social service coordinator at the WC, herself a (VM) graduate of the college credits the organization with giving her to 'courage' to do a range of things including think about taking English language classes in the city (the idea of which seemed to have been only a fantasy in the past). As she puts it:

I'll tell you something about me today. You know in the past whenever there was an argument or a fight, I used to be afraid. Even the slightest conflict and I would be scared and today in the bus I was able to stand up for myself when this man began an argument with me about my seat. I think it is because the NSS has given me exposure; I meet a lot of people on my projects. Now what I want to do is really improve my English; earlier, I wouldn't have felt I could do that. (FI, 13: 2)

Not all instances of opposition are obvious. A large amount of student struggle and negotiation is also quite subtle, especially in classrooms. Because I generally sat at the back of class, I was privy to a lot of student 'backchat', where students among themselves would respond to the teaching by imitating the teachers' English, snickering among themselves about his/her pronunciation and making fun of other students (especially enthusiastic ones sitting in the front seats) that tried to respond to teachers' questions in English. In several instances, especially when they did not know who I was (many, for a long time, assumed I was an older, returning student), they tried to include me in this 'backchat' both in class and outside it. My general silence on the issue, which seemed often to be interpreted as compliance, made me privy to many interesting comments. Students who did try to respond to teachers in English were regarded as 'high and mighty' ('She thinks too high up there' [*bahut oonchi samaj thi hain apne aap ko*], Field notes, 30 July, 2001). The pronunciation of particular English words would send some of them into giggling fits ('How do they even twist the tongue around to make such sounds, that's what I don't understand' [*Muh mein jeeb kaise marod the hain, voh hi samaj nahin aata*]).

Other ways by which the Vernacular–English gulf is bridged is by deliberate efforts made by instructors to draw on the Vernacular backgrounds of students (Canagarajah, 1999a,b). While the institution studied in detail in Chapter 5 is strongly oriented in its policies regarding this and other Vernacular-related issues, some faculty members at both colleges studied in this chapter find small ways to integrate the Vernacular into their English teaching. One literature professor spoke animatedly about reaching into Hindu myths (which most students in her class were familiar with) when discussing a poem about how life's choices can lead to unanticipated problems and how in problems are glimpses of salvation. The following excerpt is taken from her interview:

> See I try to draw them in by talking about what they know already. Regarding this poem we were doing, I asked them to think about Shiva and Parvati and the event about churning the ambrosia by the gods in the sea. Shiva arrives at the event late and by the time he gets there the ambrosia is all gone. What's left is only poison. Shiva does not want to go back to Parvati empy-handed, so he drank the poison and his throat turned blue. When he got home, Parvati says 'What did you bring?' and Shiva replies 'I have turned into Neelkanth, and have brought back my blue throat to you'. You know, it is important for them to get a sense of where they can reach or the choices that life brings them and their own [Vernacular] backgrounds can help them see that. I was telling them that the message of the poem we were doing is that you never know where a journey begins and where it ends up, just as Shiva never knew that he would return to Parvati with a blue throat. (FI, 19: 1)

While this instructor too, like some of the others at the WC, voices unhappiness about the pressures the young women bring with them, she is quick to point to the positive: 'Sometimes I do have students that will come into class completely unaware of their interest in a subject that they might actually enjoy...And then they end up doing really well, coming first in the university or first in BA or MA and then they go on for an MPhil and PhD'. This instructor also draws active parallels between Vernacular and western literatures. As she says:

> See, I begin with what they already know, and that is Gujarati. For most of these students, Gujarati is their mother-tongue. And once they have learned to appreciate Gujarati literature, once I have re-awakened their interest in stories in their mother-tongue, other kinds of literature open

up. Slowly, I get them reading English literary texts, and we draw connections. Recently, I assigned *Sophie's Choice* and they really really loved it. We worked really hard and at the end of it, one of them talked to me about what she had learned from this text and the Gujarati novel we had just finished, about how complex life's choices are and we cannot make simple judgements about where people end up in their lives. I almost cried when she said that. For an 18 year old to say that with feeling meant that something in our class had clicked. Just sparks like that make everything in this place worthwhile…Some of these students, by the time they come to the second year have become more thoughtful and by their final year are genuinely interested…I am convinced we have to start with Gujarati [the Vernacular] and move outward from there. Imposing English from the outside is not going to do anything for them, except make them more frustrated. (FI, 19: 1)

Reaching into the Vernacular background of the students seems to be what some instructors at the BC do as well, except that they do so outside class, since this institution – unlike other EM institutions in the city – has an 'English only' policy in classrooms. One economics teacher had this to say about helping the VM students with writing essay-length responses in his class:

Sometimes, I can see that they have not understood a particular concept in Economics; if they get a full essay question on it in the examination, they will really have a hard time. So I explain things in the textbooks to them in Gujarati outside class. At least in the examinations they are not worried about correct grammar and all that. If I can communicate the facts, then at least they will be able to write something. So I explain the written text in Gujarati. Some of them will actually show me their writing. I can help them when they do that. (FI, 3: 1)

Apart from this, the school also directly works on the English language fluency of their VM students by offering special courses for those students whose spoken skills are problematic. The BC recently hired an English language instructor who was himself a VM student to coordinate the extra classes for these students, and encourage his attendance at communicative language teaching workshops offered in the city. This person is also in charge of incoming VM students and has systematically tried to admit more of them. Although he has come under some criticism for doing so – since the other teachers in the school have trouble teaching VM students, especially given that they are not allowed to use the Vernacular in class – he has resisted capitulating to pressure ('The [VM] students met the criteria the college laid out; on what grounds do I tell them that even if their scores are good and spoken English is good that he or she cannot join?' [FI, 19: 4]).

Moving into the Bigger Picture: Power in Policy and Practice

Several dominant strains underlie the related dilemmas revealed by this comparative exploration including ways in which power is embedded in the ridges and caveats of the larger English–Vernaculars enterprise: between language policies and mediums of instruction (Dua, 1994; Khubchandani, 1995; Pattanayak, 1990), between class-related pressures and pedagogic practices and between teachers' expectations and student goals. Embedded in this network of alignments are also constellations of class and gender that the analysis in this chapter has tangentially touched upon. I would like, in this section, to address some of these issues.

At the level of the pedagogical practice, the issue of power seems to work itself out in terms of (mis)matches between what students have been socialized into at home and K–12 and what is expected of them in college. The VM English literature students at the WC illustrate this best in their struggle with western culture, content and English in their texts, on the one hand, and the VM practices through which these texts are taught, on the other. Canagarajah (1999b) points out the importance for all teachers to incorporate the Vernacular into the ELTL enterprise to enable (VM) students to relax about their inhibitions about learning English and also actively to communicate to students the value of their home languages. The efforts made by teachers in both colleges to bridge the English–Vernacular gulf has the social consequence of empowering groups of peoples: 'Students retain their Vernacular to a greater extent…the educational domain serves to develop and expand…and the social and educational currency of local languages is expanded' (Canagarajah, 1999b: 212). While these may be small steps to 'contest the global hegemony of English' (Canagarajah, 1999b: 212), they are necessary and important ones that need to be acknowledged and encouraged.

About the constellations of gender and class: both institutions represent two ends of a class-related spectrum and the notion of (em)power(ment) works differently in both. The WC has dedicated teachers recognizing that the area that needs most work is the self-esteem of their students if they (students) are eventually to access mainstream social goods. Empowerment for this group of students is, thus, complexly embedded partially because teachers have had to find backdoor approaches to reaching out to their students, whether it is by using Vernacular pedagogic practices or by chan-neling student interests in non-classroom-related issues. The (largely middle-class) women at the BC, however, seem to convey greater degrees of agency in terms of articulating goals for graduate study and careers. Although it can be argued that the discipline-specific nature of the business degree makes the business students more career-oriented – where a bachelor's degree in business management is seen to have better job prospects than a liberal arts BA – the fact remains that the students at the business school come equipped with the assumptions nexus that gives them access to the BC in the first place.

Medium of instruction, then, is only one social cog indexing very different social worlds, with divergent ways of producing and consuming knowledge. While the degree to which the Vernacular is embedded is relative, being more heightened in some contexts than in others, the fact remains that the Vernacular informs ELTL realities in a range of local ways in multilingual contexts that are not necessarily apparent in Anglophone countries. Indeed, they were not necessarily that apparent even to me who is from such a context, until I began the endeavor in earnest. Also not immediately apparent is the role of English – and its accompanying nexus – in sustaining the English–Vernacular chasm. Given the ever-important role that English plays in the surge toward globalization, it is particularly important that those of us in the (English) language teaching profession be mindful of how the very profession in which we are engaged perpetuates unequal power relations between entire groups of people and what we can do as teachers in small and not-so-small ways to mitigate divisions (Ramanathan, 2002a). It is equally important for us as researchers to uncover with as holistic an orientation as possible how embedded language teaching and learning practices are in the language policies, pedagogical practices and social conventions of peoples, institutions and cultures. As one of the VM students at the BC points out, 'Once you are in an English medium colleges, then what worries do you have?' [*Bus ek baar English-medium college mein admission mila, tho phir kya phikar?*] (SI, 3: 4), a quote that at once reveals that nothing about English or Vernacular knowledge production and consumption is apolitical. (But then, nothing about the researching process is either.)

I end this chapter with an extended quote:

> To rephrase Jeremy Bentham's well-known statement on the 'agenda of the state', what is the hidden agenda behind education as a social enterprise, as a system maintenance mechanism in a given social formation? As soon as you face this question you are in an area of contestation between the hegemonized and the hegemons, between ideologies promoting system stability and adversarial ideologies, between those

who possess the power to provide and control education and those who are the recipients. In this problematique one can appropriately place the contraposition of the colonial state *versus* the subject race, the colonial *versus* nationalist ideological positions, the decision-makers in education policy *versus* the recipients of education who are denied a subject role. This set of contrapositions is essentially what the contestation is about in the nationalist educational discourse. At the same time, the same problematique also accommodates a different kind of contestation: that between the privileged within Indian society (upper-caste, 'English educated', professional occupational groups) and the disprivileged (tribal groups, so-called backward castes or dalits, products of Vernacular education at best, and more often than not engaged in manual labour). The contest between nationalism in education with the colonial state is inseparably intertwined historically with the contest for hegemony within our society Sabayasachi Bhattacharya, 1998: 6).

Notes

1. The kind of study described here is similar to previous studies that have focused on local practices in particular programmes and institutions (Swales, 1998; Latour, 1996; Ramanathan, 1999), and ways in which divergent institutional cultures, when located on parallel tracks, allow the qualitative researcher to interpret one institution's norms and practices in the light of those in the other institution (Atkinson & Ramanathan, 1995; Ramanathan *et al.*, 2001).
2. Another Gujarat-specific educational policy, and one that is specifically addressed in Chapter 6, has to do with tracking practices at the college level. VM students in their highschool years are given the option of choosing English as an elective for their 10th, 11th and 12th grades or of dropping it in favor of another subject (typically accounting or typing). This means that there are two streams of VM students making their way in colleges: those who have had English from grades 5–12 (often tracked into the a-stream) and those who have had it only from grades 5–9 (typically placed into the b-stream). Other states vary in when they introduce English in VM schools. As recently as June 2000, New Delhi passed a bill that would now introduce English in Hindi-medium schools at the first grade instead of the fifth.
3. Many universities will have potential students take an entrance examination.
4. VM students get tracked into a- and b-streams, depending on their years of English instruction in school. At the college level, the university's syllabus for both tracks seem to be the same. The key items that are covered during the year in the second-year English compulsory classes are:

A-stream	B-stream
Text: *Great Expectations* (abridged version)	Text: *English prose reader* (a compilation of short stories)
Reading/comprehension Reading comprehension of job ads/sale and purchase of products Comprehension of factual and inferential questions	*Reading and comprehension:* Comprehension of advertisements for jobs/sales and purchase of products Comprehension of short news items of general interest *Comprehension above would be tested by two types of questions: 1) factual and 2) inferential questions
Writing Being able to take down main points of a given passage Letters, personal letters of greeting, of thanks, of accepting, and declining invitations, of regrets. of condolence etc.	*Writing:* Noting the main points of a given passage Letter: personal letters of greetings, thanks, accepting, and declining invitations, of regret, condolence etc.
Speaking: Division of word into syllables Accent on syllables in individual words	*Speaking accent:* Division of words into syllables Accent
Usage of idiomatic English, including phrases such as: 1) to give up, 2) to keep up, 3) to go into action, 4) to keep well, 5) to break down, 6) to go well, 7) to break out, 8) to wake up, 9) to look into, 10) to set off….	*Grammar and usage:* specific items to be identified in idiomatic usage (refer to SY a-stream syllabus)
Vocabulary: Word building, forming words with prefixes or suffixes One word substitutes Multiple choice questions Antonyms and synonyms	*Vocabulary:* Word building with prefixes and suffixes One word substitutes Antonym–synonym
Note: the teaching and testing will be at the intermediate level b-stream	*Note*: The teaching and testing will be at the elementary level

On paper, except for the fact that the two classes require different kinds of texts, the only discernable difference seems to be the note at the bottom of the each syllabus, indicating that the teaching and testing for a-stream students will at the intermediate level and for b-stream students be at the elementary level. However, nowhere is it made clear what 'elementary' *versus* 'intermediate' testing entails.

5. These degrees include a government-funded bachelor's degree in Commerce (BCom), a self-financed BCom degree, a government-funded Masters in Business Administration (MBA), and a self-financed MBA.

6. The cut-off admission score at the 12th grade for the self-financed BBA degree is lower than it is for the government-funded BCom, for instance. The government-funded degrees, are still, by and large, considered the more prestigious and competitive degrees, while privately funded degrees, because they are newer, have not yet been able to establish enough of a reputation.

7.   The economics instructor did say that he sometimes had to explain sophisti-
      cated economic concepts in Hindi to the VM students.
8.   The English and Sanskrit classes had 8–10 such interactions, as opposed to an
      average of two such interactions per class in the content-area classes.
9.   I should note here that not all EM institutions encourage independent
      thinking. The use of study guides and 'ready-made answers' which charac-
      terize the WC are common in varying degrees in other EM institutions in the
      city as well.
10.   When asked if their brothers faced similar pressures, several of the women
      said it varied. While, on the one hand, their brothers had fewer rules in general
      (*'ladka hai, tho maa-baap unke peeche nahi padthe hain'* [he's a boy, so my parents
      are not after him so much]; on the other, they also had pressures of making an
      income in ways that the females students at the WC did not have.
11.   All five of them are in their late twenties to early thirties, and, for most of
      them, this is their first job. Only one of the five had previously taught in a low-
      income college and seemed cognizant of some of the differences in the starting
      points of the students.
12.   The University Grants Commission requires college students to participate in
      one of three options: (1) service in the NSS, (2) physical training or (3) sports.

Chapter 5

The Divisive Politics of Tracking

It is August 16 (1998), a day after the Indian Independence Day. I sit in the Vice-Principal's office talking to him about state-mandated policies around tracking VM students into separate 'streams' based on the number of years of English instruction they have had in school. This college has over the last 7–8 years, unlike other colleges in the city, institutionalized the practice of reserving one of the streams only for Dalit students. I have known this Jesuit priest all my life; he was a key figure in my life when I was growing up. I did my undergraduate studies at this institution, and while much of the college is the same, much of it has changed. These tracking practices are certainly new. Father A. looks at me and says 'Vaidehi, we have chosen to have an open-door policy for all Dalit students that apply. It wasn't a policy when you were here. It has become our way of interpreting "social justice" and of "bringing all to the table".' When I asked him if the institution faced resistance regarding this policy, his response became more political: 'We are at a stage now in our development as a country [51 years since the end of The Raj] where we are waking up to the specific choices we can make about equity. We don't just have to go along with what was passed down to us. The one sentiment that kept getting echoed all through last year during the 50th Independence anniversary was that we definitely now can articulate our own practices. It's a matter of pride now, isn't it?'
And I think to myself: Can we ever address education, language policies, religion, politics, ideologies separately from each other?
Look at the interconnections here!
(Field notes, 16 August 1998, 2.30p.m.)

Previous research on tracking (Anyon, 1997; Shuman, 1985) has shown how language proficiency can serve as a gate-keeping measure that determines ways in which students can gain access to particular avenues to which they may seek entry. In many cases, mastery over the standard variety of a language (Gee, 1990) or over particular academic registers serves as a tool by which students' intelligence and aptitude are assessed, tools that often have the unfortunate effect of slotting students into damaging grooves. In the Indian socio-educational context, such tracking measures can be seen to feed into the English–Vernacular chasm. To make the English–Vernacular canvas more nuanced, this chapter will address some prominent tracking-related features. Some of these have to do with the nature and general justification for tracking; others have to do with the consequences of these measures for different groups of students. While the general points regarding tracking issues are applicable for most VM students in the city, I address these issues in one particular institutional context that has recently adopted a highly activist orientation. Attempting to understand how the socially stratifying practice of tracking functions in an institutional context that is trying to be markedly resistant and critical in its overall endeavor allows us to understand some complex ways in which resistance functions. Indeed, the institution discussed here attempts to address the inequalities inherent in the tracking system by both working with it and simultaneously giving it a critical twist. As I will attempt to point out, while some (classroom) practices can be seen to maintain the English–Vernacular gulf, there are others that serve as bridges.

A key social issue that this college is committed to addressing in as many realms of its institutional realities as possible is caste inequality. This institution has, in recent years, made active and deliberate efforts at bridging the English–Vernacular gulf by reaching out to a particular group of disadvantaged VM students, namely *Dalit* (low-caste) students and students from so called 'Other Backward Classes',[1] by ensuring that one of its 'tracks' is devoted exclusively to this group of students. Addressing how some tracking-related issues that inform VM students in other colleges are resonant with the experiences of VM Dalit students in this particular institution is valuable, since these issues simultaneously shed light on both the EM–VM divide in general as well as local efforts at countering dominating alignments (Ramanathan, 2002b). An understanding of how this particular institution wrestles with common state-wide language policies, on the one hand, while not losing sight of its specific long-term activist cause, on the other, affords a fuller understanding of the fact that resistance efforts at opposing perceived 'dominant structures' in some domains co-exist with compliance and conformity in others.

I should, at this point, insert a note about my acute discomfort in writing parts of this chapter, some of which have to do with caste issues, others with juxtaposing my insider–outsider role and I would like to address them. Readers may find my discussion of caste 'thin'. Indeed, I find it 'thin'. There are both personal and societal reasons for this. Part of my discomfort – the personal – stems from my own privileged caste status – as indicated partly by my last name, since all Hindu last names supposedly index caste positionings – that I really took for granted. I am a Tamilian Brahmin and it is with a lot of trepidation (and shame, given the historical atrocities and colonization associated with this caste category) that I even acknowledge this. Certainly, in India, I would not ever overtly mention my caste background. But since I am writing for a largely western audience, and because this chapter addresses issues related to caste and because I feel it is imperative that the 'researcher' assume a self-reflexive position, I feel the pressure to mention my caste positioning. I have to say that I grew up with very little real sense of how caste dynamics work largely because my parents, staunchly anti-caste-ist in their orientation, refused to let that be a filter through which my brother and I saw the world. While this was most valuable in my growing years, I feel that it left me ill equipped to fully understand and capture the nuances of caste negotiations, especially as they occurred in this college setting. As for the societal reason, there is a lot of silence and hesitation around discussing caste issues in public in India. A lot of middle-class Indians like myself worry about seeming 'caste-ist' by even raising the issue in conversations. Certainly, it was uppermost in my mind during my interactions with students at this college and I found I could not bring myself to ask them caste-related questions. The people at this institution who did talk about it were the priests and some of the faculty. However, even some of those interactions were dissatisfactory. Despite knowing that caste is a most complex, socially stratifying term, with sub-castes within each other, the priests too seemed uncomfortable with delineating it beyond 'Dalit' (explained presently) and 'Other Backward Classes'. Their commitment to reaching out to this group of peoples, though, remains resolute and undeterred.

The other issue of discomfort has to do with my role in this college. In many ways, the 'insider' aspects of my role as 'researcher' were heightened in this institution because this was the college in which I studied for my undergraduate degree. The classrooms, hallways, bulletin boards and canteens were my old haunts. Many of the priests that run this college are people I have known for many years. It is with some embarrassment that I acknowledge how little I really knew then of what VM students in the same college went through. Although some of these students were my friends and although the practice of tracking that this college and other colleges in the state have to follow was instituted after I graduated, in retrospect I feel I had only an inkling of their education-related conflicts and ambiguities, most of which revolved around clashes between the teaching and learning of English in this EM college and their VM backgrounds. If my voice in this chapter is more uneven than in the others, it is because I am genuinely struggling between my insider–outsider positions.

Hegemony, Caste, Discrimination and Social Justice: Some General Connections

The institution under discussion in this chapter is run by the Jesuit community based in the city. The priests who run the school have, in recent years, committed themselves to helping the most disadvantaged of VM students, namely those who fall under the 'Dalit' and 'other backward classes' 'categories' under the auspices of their doctrine of 'social justice'. These terms – Dalit, 'Other Backward Classes (OBCs)' and social justice – are complex terms and, at the risk of hugely simplifying them, I would like, in this section, to address how they come together in this particular institutional context. Doing so should elucidate the complex endeavor in which this institution is engaged.

Hegemonic practices, as Gramsci (1988) maintains, are repressive practices in any given social structure that ensure that the means and ownership of production remain in the hands of a few. These practices are perpetuated at every stratum of society by a variety of invisible factors aligning with each other – including institutions, religions and legal practices – that justify unequal distributions of goods (Gee, 1990) and disallow minority groups access to and ownership of the means of production. The construct of caste and its entailing social practices in India exemplify hegemonic practices that are historically and currently associated with keeping Dalit and OBCs in disadvantaged positions (Sarkar, 1984). Castes are hierarchically arranged social units based on traditional occupations and, as endogamous groups (i.e. marrying within the caste), they function to preserve the social stratification by inhibiting mobility between castes. Caste endogamy is still almost practiced (except amongst a small section of a westernized élite) even though traditional caste occupations are not necessarily followed.[2] The following is a (very) simplified breakdown of castes according to the *Varnasharma* (the caste system): Brahmins (or priests), Kshatriyas (or warriors), Vaishyas (or traders) and Sudras (or service castes, who the constitution today refers to as 'other backward classes') (for fuller explanations, see Quigley [1993] and Dirks [2001]). People of a Dalit background, as they are named in the Constitution, are outside the caste system altogether. Since Independence, these people are the beneficiaries of affirmative action programmes set in place in the Indian Constitution. The term by which they now prefer to be called (rejecting Gandhi's word for them *'Harijan'* (which meant Children of God)) is *Dalit*, meaning 'crushed/oppressed'.

Although this conceptualization of caste in India is, at best, a drastic simplification and, at worst, misleading, it has remained singularly resistant to modification. The discussion of caste is often framed within two mutually exclusive conceptions of history: materialist *versus* idealist (Quigley, 1993). According to the former view, caste is simply a rationalization and obfuscation of more basic inequalities: those higher on the caste scale are generally wealthier than those who are lower. In hegemonic terms, the higher castes have more access to the means of production, including better schooling, better jobs and more social goods. The idealist position, however, maintains that caste is a cultural construct and that people are placed higher or lower on the scale based on religiously sanctioned notions of purity and impurity. From such a point of view, 'material considerations are largely irrelevant because caste is essentially an ideological framework for explaining universal problems of social order...where the structure of caste is to be found in a system of ideas and not in concrete manifestation of those ideas' (Quigley, 1993: 3).

The general stance on caste adopted in this chapter is that both the materialist and idealist positions are relevant. While I was intellectually aware of this, the ways in which it materially manifested itself on the ground made me sharply aware of how deep caste and caste distinctions run. While caste may not be as much of an issue for 'upper-caste' Hindus such as myself, I only had to be in conversation with some of the Jesuit priests of this college who are tackling the caste issue head-on to realize that my understanding of how caste dynamics played out in the classroom, in institutional orientations and in language policies was most myopic. The material aspects of castes have been historically present and are still evident in several spheres of existence in India, most especially in the lack of opportunities for upward mobility for those that identify themselves as 'Dalit' or 'other backward classes'. Although India has adopted and reinforced a strong affirmative action policy whereby slots ('seats') are reserved for these people in several realms of living – including education and employment – discrimination against them still exists (Kamble, 1983; Sarkar, 1984). The idealist perspective of caste, I found, operates more at an ideological level with discriminatory practices that categorize some people as pure and the rest as impure.

The Catholic institution under discussion in the present chapter is one that I attended as an undergraduate. When I began this overall project several years ago, it seemed natural to begin it in this setting. However, much has changed in the college from the time I graduated (1985), including those issues relating to curriculum, university-mandated tracking practices and its overall pro-Vernacular stance. The activist stance that the college now assumes is very visible, with its social justice policy now directly oriented to addressing the college needs of those VM students who are simultaneously poor and of Dalit backgrounds. Recognizing that the 'call to serve' has undergone transformations over the years, the Society of Jesus has articulated an extended set of statements on its new dimensions of justice. The following excerpts taken from the 34th General Congregation of the Society of Jesus provide a partial orientation to this institution's stance toward these students:

> The struggle for justice has a progressive and gradually unfolding historic character, as it confronts the changing needs of specific peoples, cultures and times. Previous Congregations have called attention to the need to work for structural changes in the socio-economic and political orders as an important dimension of the promotion of justice. They also urged: working for peace and reconciliation through non-violence; working to end discrimination against people based on race, religion, gender, ethnic background or social class; working to counter growing poverty and hunger while material prosperity becomes ever more concentrated. Each of us may focus efforts in only one of other dimensions, but all of them are of continuing importance in the society's overall mission in the promotion of justice…
>
> In our times there is a growing consciousness of the interdependence of all peoples in one common heritage. The globalization of the world economy and society proceeds at a rapid pace, fed by developments in technology, communication, and business. While this phenomenon can produce many benefits, it can also result in injustices on a massive scale: economic adjustment programmes and market forces unfettered by concern for their social impact, especially on the poor; the homogenous 'modernization' of cultures in ways that destroy traditional cultures and values; a growing inequality among nations and – within nations – between rich and poor, between the powerful and marginalized. In justice we must counter this by working to build up a world order of genuine solidarity where all can have a rightful place at the banquet of the Kingdom…
>
> *Indigenous peoples* in many parts of the world, isolated and relegated to marginal social roles, see their identity, cultural legacy and natural world threatened. Other social groups – an example would be the *Dalits*, considered 'untouchables' in some parts of South Asia – suffer severe social discrimination in civil even ecclesiastical society. The General Congregation calls on the whole Society to renew its long-standing commitment to such peoples.
>
> The Society continues to insist on the promotion of justice. Why? Because it corresponds to our very spirituality…The promotion of justice signifies a call for the Society to insert ourselves even more profoundly

in the concrete lives of peoples and nations – as they actually are and not as we think they ought to be.

As these excerpts indicate, reaching out to the poorer segments of a society is a central tenet of the 'social justice' doctrine and one way in which Catholic institutions have done so has been in the realm of education (Heredia, 2000), where schools are not seen as 'agents of evangelization, but rather in terms of a theology of secular action and involvement' (D'souza, 1994: 134). Schools founded and run by Christian missionaries are acknowledged to be the best in the country and admission to these is greatly sought after. They have produced (and continue to produce) the nation's élite. Catholic educational institutions, specifically Jesuit institutions, have engaged in a great deal of reflection regarding the élitist nature of their schools and colleges.[3] D'souza (1994) stresses the need for Catholic education to remember how it began. Catholic education is so sought after today in India that we forget that 'Christian institutions which began as orphanages, today appear as high class boarding schools, so restrictive in admissions that there is no place for the poor in the inn' (D'souza, 1994: 119). Toward partially addressing this charge and recommitting itself to its faith, the institution under discussion holds 'social justice' as central to its general orientation. Figure 5.1 shows the four dimensions of this term (taken from Mwijage, 2002: 2).

No service of faith without: promotion of justice entry into cultures openness to other religious experiences	No enculturation without: communicating faith with others dialogue with other traditions commitment to justice
No promotion of justice without: communicating faith transforming cultures collaboration with other traditions	No dialogue without: sharing faith with others evaluating cultures concern for justice

Figure 5.1 The four dimensions of social justice

Relating these views to Ignation charity where faith and charity are to have social dimensions, social justice informs 'the chief purpose of the Society of Jesus today, in that the Society should strive not only for its own salvation and perfection, but for that of its neighbour as well...' (Mwijage, 2002: 2). As the principal of the college explains it, 'this doctrine can be adapted according to their mission in the world' (FI, 7: 1). Put differently, it was a matter of finding the seeds in the kingdom of God and then collaborating in the transformation of the world' (Albrecht, 2002). The policy of doing whatever it could to help Dalit students became, for this institution, one way in which to put their social justice doctrine to practice.[4] The institution has, in recent years, committed itself to empowering them in a variety of non-academic and academic ways. In the area of extra-curricular support, the institution assists in organizing regular group meetings wherein Dalits share their experiences with discrimination and think about avenues for change. Toward taking their messages to the community, the groups also practice and organize street plays. (Indeed, one such meeting called *Ahmedabad Ekta* [United Ahmedabad] partially supported by this college became so well known that many 'non-Dalits' began to join.)

In the realm of academic support, the college has an open-door policy regarding admission for these students.[5] To help them adjust to the demands of college-level instruction, the institution offers them extra-curricular support during their first year in the form of tutorials in the English language, an area in which these students need a great deal of help (addressed in detail later in the chapter). The college also has a reputation of being one of the premier EM colleges in the state with several of its departments including biochemistry, English, Sanskrit and economics being recognized as strong departments that were active in research and that students graduated with top marks in university final examinations. In recent years, however, the institution's academic standards were thought to have gone down slightly because it admits Dalit and OBC students who have not done as well as the other students in their 12th grade examinations.[6]

According to the vice principal of the college, an average of 1500 students are enrolled at any given time. Of these, 500–600 students are enrolled in the arts and the remaining in the sciences. Approximately 375 of the arts students come from VM schools and more than half of this number (56–60%) are Dalit. The number of students admitted each year from this group in both the arts and the sciences has increased steadily because of the Jesuit Community's commitment to 'serve the poor and the oppressed' (FI, 4: 2).

How State-wide Tracking Practices Work in This Institution

Instituted after I graduated, I found that the college, like other colleges in the state, had to follow university-wide mandates[7] to track VM students entering EM colleges. VM students are tracked into different 'steams' depending on the years of English they have had through their K–12 schooling. Because VM students have the option of 'dropping' English after the ninth grade, there is one set of students that arrives at the (EM) college scene having had only five years of English instruction (from grades 5–9). This set of students is tracked into the b-stream. Those VM students that have had English from grade 5 get placed into the a-stream.[8] Students in the a-stream are assumed to have a moderate grasp on the language and are, according to the *Teacher's Handbook* issued by the central university, placed at the intermediate level. Most a-stream students are generally from middle-class homes and their literacy levels in Gujarati are relatively high; b-stream students, in contrast, come from farming communities outside Ahmedabad and most have attended municipal schools. Mainstream Gujarati is, in some instances, an L2 or second dialect, with English constituting a third (sometimes fourth) language.

B-stream students in this Jesuit college (but not necessarily in other colleges) are primarily Dalit students with rural backgrounds and it is primarily in this way that this institution partially begins to address some caste-related inequalities. The general understanding of the managerial staff is that the problems represented and encountered by these students are complex and that the English–Vernacular gulf they experience is a surface manifestation of a range of other issues. The principal maintains that it is necessary to provide welcoming, non-threatening access to the same goods that EM students automatically assume during their time in the college. The special English language instruction provided to these students (addressed specifically toward the end of this chapter) is to be partially understood against this general rationale (see Table 5.1).

Table 5.1 Placement of students in English Compulsory classes

Student's K–12 medium	Division	Prior English language instruction	Stream (EC placement)
Gujarati	A	Grades 5–12	a
		Grades 5–9	b
English	B	n.a.	None

The English language experiences of both a- and b-stream students will inform the following sections. Where relevant I will make comparisons to their EM counterparts. As we will see, both sets of students have divergent English language experiences (experiences that resonate with other VM students in EM colleges). While none of the interviewed students ostensibly articulated any resentment at being tracked into a- and b-streams in the college (since this tracking was seen as a consequence of an 'individual' choice to continue or to stop taking English in grades 10–12,[9] many did admit to feeling intense pressure to 'drop' English after the ninth grade. Several said that fear of not doing well in English in the 10th and 12th grade Board examinations and worries about not getting into a 'good' college kept them from opting for it[10] and many attributed their general fear of English to poor, inadequate English instruction in their rural, municipal schools (*'arre, school teacher ko bhi English baat karne mein mushkil hoti hai…'* [Even the school teachers have trouble speaking English…] [SI, 5: 1]).

This practice of tracking VM students into a- and b-streams then, although justified by the state on the basis of students' divergence in English proficiency, can be seen to build on their already disadvantaged position especially when we consider their predicament two years into college: in the third and final year of college, all a-stream, b-stream and EM students have to take the same English language examination. Needless to say, b-stream students are ill prepared to do so. Not only have they been socialized into less powerful cultural models of literacy at the K–12 realm, their condition is further exacerbated by being slotted into invisible, institutionalized grooves such as the streams previously mentioned. As we will presently see, the English language experiences of b-stream (VM) students are similar to those at the women's college (in terms of pedagogic practices and general desire for English fluency) and, in this sense, more representative of the English–Vernacular divide. In other instances, though, particular pedagogic practices in this institutional context can be seen as efforts to bridge the English–Vernacular gulf. The classroom practice of two-way translation (Naregal, 2001), for instance, explained at length later, is a case in point. Extremely complex and sometimes contradictory, then, I have tried to capture, as fully as possible, the divergently pulled strings and have tried to resist massaging 'data' to prove a point. While this sometimes makes for incongruous messages – as indeed sections of this chapter will indicate – in other ways, it allows us to see how the larger socio-educational scene is rife with clashing, paradoxical moments that remain inexplicable to both me as a 'relative insider/outsider' and to participants in the socio-educational system itself.

Tracking Practice 1: English Language Experiences of B-Streamers

Extensive use of translation

If teachers at the women's college teach almost entirely in the Vernacular, the language teachers of VM students at this college teach in a combination of Gujarati and English, resorting to extensive translating, especially in *b*-stream classes. (As one who was in the EM track of this college 20 years ago, I do not remember such translation practices in the EM.) Indeed, an instructor who does not translate enough or who tends to use more English in class is generally seen as more difficult to understand and was not, in general, regarded as a good teacher ('*Gujarati ane Hindi nathi vaparthi, ane amne mushkil laage cche*' [She doesn't use either Gujarati or Hindi and we find that difficult], [SI, 19: 3]). Teachers, for their part, feel that they have to use the native languages because it has become a way to engage the students and 'to get through to them' (FI, 5: 4), especially because b-stream students have not studied English after the ninth grade.

Most everything in b-stream classes – directives, vocabulary, entire paragraphs from short stories – is first read in English and then translated and explained in Gujarati. Teachers frequently called on students to read a passage aloud from their textbooks and then have them translate it into Gujarat or Hindi as a way to check comprehension. Two-way translations serve other purposes as well: by using Vernaculars, teachers were not only drawing on resources students brought with them to class – thus validating their home identities and discourses – but also proactively partially working to reduce the pressure students feel to engage in extensive memorizing. As one teacher in the VM college put it:

> If I have them translate what I have said or what they read back into Gujarati, then I know they have understood. This helps a lot. I do think that if they understand what they are reading, they are less likely to simply parrot all the stuff. (FI, 15: 2)

Recalling the points made about how ideologies percolate down to classrooms, views like these seem to invoke actively Gandhi's points regarding 'foreign' education encouraging 'imitators' and 'crammers'. The following quote from Gandhi's ideas on the 'foreign' *versus* Vernacular education partially illustrates the connections:

> The foreign medium has caused brain fag, put undue strain upon the nerves of our children, made them crammers and imitators, unfitted them for original work and thought, and disabled them for filtrating

their learning to the family or the masses. The foreign medium has made our children practically foreigners in their own land. It is the greatest tragedy of the existing system. The foreign medium has prevented the growth of our Vernaculars. If I had the powers of a despot, I would today stop the tuition of our boys and girls through a foreign medium, and require all the teachers and professors on pain of dismissal to introduce the change forthwith. I would not wait for the preparation of textbooks. They will follow the change… . (Gandhi, *Young India,* 1 September 1921)

The use of translation extends to directions in grammar workbooks as well. The reverse process also seems popular, with teachers explaining points in Gujarati and having students translate them back to them in English. When asked if using Gujarati or Hindi in the classroom hindered their English language learning, all students unequivocally maintained that it helped: drawing on the Vernacular helped them understand (*'na hi tho naa samjan padeh'* [otherwise I won't understand], [SI, 8: 1]) just as the translating helped them make constant connections between Gujarat and English. For the teachers, translation serves to bridge the gap between the Vernacular and target language.

Emphasis on grammar

While two-way translations are small ways by which the English–Vernacular gulf is bridged in classrooms, the relatively heavy emphasis on grammar seems to maintain the gulf. Almost all instruction in the first-year b-stream classes, for instance, are devoted exclusively to the teaching of grammar. The class instructor felt that such intensive attention was warranted because 'the students' hold on grammar and the basics was so poor' (FI, 4: 6) that he felt could proceed with the readings in the textbooks only after he had addressed all the necessary grammar points. Thus, classroom instruction in the English Compulsory (EC) classes was generally devoted to various grammatical features, with tenses taught in one class, nouns in the next and verbs in the class after. The following extract is culled from my field notes from one such class. I have interspersed some of the teachers' utterances (denoted by T) into my field notes; note that the teacher gave all of the instructions in Gujarati and English.

T: *Homework kone karayu?* Who has done the homework?
      *[Teacher asked how many of the students have done the assigned homework; goes over drill on negative forms that he had assigned in the previous class.]
T: Overcome *etle suu?*
      *[Goes over different meanings of *to overcome* to succeed, to master.]

T: *Aaje ame tenses karvaana chhe.* We will do tenses today. *[Says they are going to do tenses today and that they have to memorize the rules, says this thrice: 'There is no other way of learning the rules'.]

T: *Badhuj gokhi kaado.* Memorize them all by heart. *[Lays out the following three columns on the board]:

Present	Past	Past participle
Leave	Left	Left
Complete	Completed	Completed
Forget	Forgot	Forgotten

*[Continues this list in the next class, where again he reiterates the importance of memorizing these lists.] (Field notes, 22 June, 1997)

Equally strong emphasis on discrete units of language was evident in the a-stream classes, although the focus in these classes seemed less on sentence-level units than on paragraph-level features (e.g. students reordered jumbled sentences into the correct order).

When asked, all of the VM students – a- and b-streamers – said that this almost exclusive attention to grammar helped them to speak correctly but did not really prepare them to use English in contexts like job interviews ('*Amne to ahinya grammaraj sikhwaade cheh; English maa vaat karvani practice tho nathi malthu…tho job interview maa mushkil hoye amne*' [We only get taught grammar here; we don't get to practice speaking English…so we find job interviews difficult] [SI, 9: 2]). Despite this, however, the generally pervasive sentiment that English is a passport to social successes in their culture prompt these students to take the grammar instruction in their EC classes seriously ('*Thoda kuch tho seekh lenge*' [At least I'll learn something] [SI, 6: 1]). As with the VM students in the women's college, all students in the a- and b-stream alike voiced the need to be able to speak English fluently, because, as one student put it, this would give them an 'impressive personality' [in English] (SI, 6: 2).

In concluding this section on pedagogical practices, then, we can see similarities between the language experiences of b-stream students at this college and the VM students at the women's college (explored in Chapter 4; see also Appendix 4). However, there appeared to be at least one significant difference between the teacher–student relationships in the two institutional settings. Almost all of the teachers at the WC could relate to the Vernacular backgrounds of their students because most of them (teachers) had been educated themselves in Gujarati. In this EM Jesuit college, however, VM students felt that their teachers – by and large educated in the English medium – could not relate to their (students') Vernacular backgrounds because many of their teachers do not really know what it is like in their home villages (*'ammeh to gaam ma thi aavya ane ahiyaan tho teacher baddha joodhi riteh sikhwaade ccheh'* [I come from the village; the teachers here teach very differently], [SI, 15: 3]).

Tracking Practice 2: English Language Experiences of EM and A-stream Students: A Preference for English Literature

While it is not my intention in this section to trace how English literature dug deep roots in Indian soil (for fuller accounts of this, see Vishwanathan [1989] and Suleri [1992]), I would like to call attention to how complexly English literature teaching is positioned not only in this institution but in the culture at large. Indeed, the neocolonial impact of English literature as an academic enterprise is only recently being seriously critiqued and decolonized (Pal *et al.,* 2001). While I majored in English literature myself from this college, some of the conflicts around it for VM students were not apparent to me because the tracking policy was not in place 20 years ago. Part of the complexity seems to be this: until quite recently, majoring in English literature – including British, US and Indian writings in English – seemed to be one of the only ways several VM students (in all colleges across the city) felt they could master the English language (see Appendix 4 for a sample English literature syllabus). Doing so in an EM college, including the one under discussion, however, is clearly not easy for this group of students. Four relevant themes emerged from the data regarding the effect of literature teaching on students' access to English. These factors, related to bureaucratic procedures, cultural practices regarding learning and areas of cultural conflict apply to all a- and b-stream students, although the implications for b-stream students are more extreme. As with the previous section on pedagogic practices, this section is not specific to this particular Jesuit college; versions of these points resonate with other EM colleges in the state. Cumulatively, they point to the general English–Vernacular divide.

Gate-keeping

Most VM students in EM colleges are not able to major in English literature, an option that is largely available to EM students in this and other EM colleges in the city. (The women's college discussed in Chapter 4, it can be recalled, is a VM college where VM students can and do major in English literature.) As one faculty member put it, 'With EM students you can at least assume a degree of language proficiency that does not make the task of teaching Chaucer and Shakespeare seem insurmountable' (FI, 2: 11). Among VM students, only a handful of exceptionally good a-stream students – at both WC and this college – were allowed to major in English but only after they had successfully passed a test administered by the English faculty. Because their English language proficiency is generally deemed poorer than that of their EM counterparts, VM a-stream students majoring in English were required to take intensive grammar, reading and written instruction in a remedial English class or tutorial. As for Dalit and 'OBC' b-stream students who dropped English after the ninth grade, majoring in English literature was not even a possibility.

English teachers' view of their role

A second important theme that emerges through the faculty interviews is that the English department faculty see themselves as literature not language teachers. All five faculty members mentioned that the language problems of the VM students were not really their responsibility and most felt at a loss at having to address grammar-related problems when teaching Chaucer and Shakespeare. All but one teacher also expressed discomfort at teaching the English language classes, where language-related concerns are addressed. Many of the faculty also believed that the college's recently adopted stance on promoting the English language skills of Dalit students seems to work at odds with the faculty's literature background and find themselves occasionally resenting the management's not fully under-standing that 'literature and language teaching are two separate endeavors' (FI, 3: 4). Both the college management and department, in response to this struggle, have recently lobbied for the introduction of a course on 'Communicative English' into the university syllabus (more on this presently),[11] which they hope would give students options that they currently do not have.

Heavy use of study guides

A third significant practice that emerged was the students' extensive use of study guides. Several of the VM a-stream students who were majoring in English literature admitted to relying heavily on such guides to get them through examinations because they felt their English language proficiency was inadequate for understanding and explaining concepts in literary theory and poetry and that study guides explained difficult literary concepts in Gujarati. (Indeed, I remember perusing some of these study guides myself, since they were so heavily oriented to the final examinations that we were all generally anxious about performing well in.) As for poetry, all of the students believed unequivocally that poetic language and metaphors (especially in contemporary poetry as opposed, for example, to the nature poetry of the romantics) were difficult to grasp. Resorting to memorizing summaries and explanations of such poetry from such guides affords them a way of dealing with possible exam questions on these topics.

Cultural dissonance

Another issue related to literature teaching was the students' feeling of cultural dissonance between themselves and the topics portrayed in the literature. Students in literature classes also voiced feelings of alienation from texts with overly western themes. When asked what sense they made of romantic love – a theme predominant in much western literature – several students admitted to sometimes being at a loss (*'mushkil laage cheh'* [it is difficult] [SI, 3: 2]), since in many parts of India's Vernacular cultures, love between the sexes tends to operate in the framework of arranged marriages. (However, current Hindi movies valorizing romantic love seem to be changing attitudes about love, relationships and marriage/s. Indeed, I remember struggling with issues of cultural dissonance too, although my own issues were perhaps not as marked as the VM students). Some students said they had come to terms with such western themes by experiencing them vicariously; others would try to translate them into local terms. Students contending with race relations in the abridged version of *Uncle Tom's Cabin,* (the required text for the third-year English language class), for example, made sense of the text by understanding it in terms of unequal power relations between castes in India (*Jaat jevi cheh?* [Is it like caste], *tho bahu power inequality cheh?* [So there is a lot of power inequality?] [SI, 6: 2]). Several students also believed that they often had to forgo dealing with some poems because certain experiences and themes were too far removed from their everyday realities or could not be culturally transposed into local terms (a theme that we saw echoed by VM students in Chapter 4).

Bridging the English–Vernacular Chasm

The 'de-voicing' tracking practices detailed here are similar to those found in other EM institutions in the city. As discussed in Chapters 3 and 4 as well as in this one, the unequal grooves in which VM and EM students find themselves are set in place very many years prior to their appearance on the college scene. Certainly, very many factors devaluing the Vernacular – from unequal cultural models, to unreasonable state-level options of dropping English after the ninth grade while insisting that they take the same college-level English examination – send out strong messages of neglect to VM students. From such points of view, the English–Vernacular chasm is clearly and sharply in focus.

I turn now to addressing how this particular college has, in recent years, worked at bridging the various gulfs (a-stream *versus* b-stream, EM *versus* VM) by actively trying to integrate the Vernaculars with English. Several institutional practices and orientations set this college apart from other EM colleges in the city. They range from deliberate changes in everyday routines in classrooms and extra-curricular activities, to changes in curricula and requirements, to advocating changes in courses at the university level, to being openly and actively committed to reserving b-stream classes for those VM students that are disadvantaged by caste and/or income.

One way in which the institution's commitment at integrating Gujarati with English is apparent is in the relatively prominent place being accorded to it in the last four to five years. The current principal of the college (who holds an MA in Linguistics from Georgetown University), schooled in the VM and a teacher of Gujarati literature, decided when he assumed office that he would do what he could to keep the institution multilingual. Thus, his speech welcoming faculty and students on the first day of the academic year – which until then was only in English – is now in Gujarati, a move he feels is truly welcoming to VM students. All written announcements on notice boards are now in Gujarati and English. He has also been careful to plan student events where EM and VM students work together. Each year the college hosts a three day cultural festival for which all students but especially VM students from all three years are encouraged to volunteer time in organizing and participating in the events. Indeed, he has appointed a faculty member from the English department who is interested in second-language issues to find ways of reaching out to VM students and involving them.

At the level of courses and curricular materials, the institution has, in recognition of the need for making English literature and English language separate enterprises, lobbied the university to start a course on 'Communicative English'. While this course has not yet been approved as a possible subject for students to major in, it has been integrated into the mainstream English syllabus. As seen from Table 5.2, the original syllabus for the course intends to be 'practical', with the explicit aim of training young men and women in various communicative skills, written and conversational.

Table 5.2 A partial syllabus of the course on Communicative English

Paper number	Name of paper
First year	
Paper 1	Introduction to phonetics
Paper 2	Remedial grammar
Paper 3	Applied phonetics
Paper 4	Remedial grammar
Second year	
Paper 5	Writing skills
Paper 6	Conversational English
Paper 7	Broadcasting (Introduction to media broadcasting)
Paper 8	Conversational English
Third year	
Paper 9	Broadcasting: radio
Paper 10	Conversational English
Paper 11	Project

Other curricular changes include offering remedial courses for VM a-stream students opting to major in English literature. The English department faculty, without monetary or any other kind of recompense, has rallied together to take turns in working on improving the writing skills of these students, by devising diagnostic tests, breaking down texts into manageable units and working on grammar-related issues as well as those related to taking examinations. These remedial classes ran for a period of five years from 1995–2000 and were conducted three times a week for incoming VM students who chose to major in English. The following extended quote captures one faculty member's summation of these classes:

While at the level of conceptualization, a unit was to be devoted to grammar, conversation, and reading comprehension, and while the format was generally followed, toward the end of the term the students would inevitably ask for (and get) help for forthcoming examinations in terms of formulated answers to expected questions. On the whole, however, the classes gave students a fair degree of confidence. As a small group entitled to special interaction with the faculty, they experienced closer bonding with the teachers, their shyness and fear of their more sophisticated peers dropped away, and they were ready to participate vocally even in the larger regular classes. Their efforts at self-expression showed marked improvement. All sorts of methods were improvised and tried out…While the literature faculty went in without any training in ELT, some proved ingenious in their impromptu methods, and were able to make the students relax and enjoy themselves, with the result that they learned faster and better. The classes had to be discontinued when shortage of staff and the opening of a graduate centre in English in the college made it impossible for the staff to bear the extra burden. Some of these students have gone on to do graduate work in English literature. (FI, 12)

Of course, a question that emerges here is: is English the way to 'opening doors'? While the institution may be leaning in this direction, it is doing so by being mindful of not losing sight of valuing what VM students bring with them. The college management, unlike those of the other two institutions, is clear about the overlapping nature of English and the Vernaculars and is committed to stressing it. However, the most crucial way in which this institution serves the VM student population is by reaching out to the most disadvantaged of this group, namely those of Dalit backgrounds, and validating their Vernacular backgrounds. While the college, like other colleges in the city, has had to struggle with working out gulfs relating to tracking practices (between both a- and b-stream students and between VM and EM students in general), it is clear in its mission to help those they feel are most in need of it. By making it a policy that their b-stream classes will be made up only of Dalit students, the institution is going against the norm of other EM colleges in the state. While this institution too wrestles with how best to teach VM students, it is going about doing so in deliberate, conscious, concerted ways. By making language and social problems issues to be thought about, critically discussed and addressed at a variety of levels, this college is keeping VM students on the 'front burner' so to speak, instead of relegating them to the back and treating them as 'non-issues'. In so doing, the college is not just making serious attempts at integrating Vernacular traditions, values and languages with the ethos of an EM college but it is, in effect, taking a critical, ethical stance that says that social justice is indeed a matter of recognizing and alleviating the needs of those the system leaves behind. In this sense, it is accomplishing its intended Catholic mission – to serve and educate those most in need of it – in a larger socio-educational system where English divides.

Notes

1. Patronizing as this term is, I am using it because it is the term used in Indian governmental parlance.
2. Caste and occupation, as Quigley (1993) points out, do not necessarily go hand in hand. Although the relationship between the two is one way of explaining the social stratification in the caste system, it is extremely outdated. Today, a person born into the tailor caste may not be locked into the tailoring profession but may simply have once had an ancestor who was a tailor.
3. Among these are St Xavier's College, Mumbai, St Xavier's College, Calcutta, and Loyola College, Chennai, all three rated among the top ten in the country, year after year.
4. Dalits who convert to Christianity lose the rights to the reserved quota earmarked for them and get classed as Other Backward Classes in Gujarat (for whom also there are some reserved seats but not as many).
5. Most institutions in the state do not have such a policy in place. Although all state- and government-funded institutions must reserve seats for students from this group, this college has chosen, in recent years, to open more than the required quota of seats as a way of generally uplifting this historically disadvantaged group.
6. In fact, Dalit and OBC students need only passing marks to gain admission into the college whereas all other students have to meet the college's cut-off score (62–64% for the arts, 65% for the sciences) on their 12th grade examinations.
7. All public colleges in the state are affiliated to Gujarat University. Mandates related to syllabi, curricula and teaching come down from the university to local colleges, a fact that many teachers – both in this college and the two others – feel constrains their autonomy.
8. All VM students – a- and b-streamers – fall into the A division. All EM students fall into the B division.
9. I question this 'choice' in Chapter 6.
10. Accounting or Typing – two other classes that GM students can opt for – are seen as subjects that are 'easy to score in', subjects where they are not expected to write essay-type responses to questions.
11. 'Communicative English' was granted to this college in 2001.

Chapter 6

Gulfs and Bridges Revisited: Hybridity, Nativization and Other Loose Ends

We see the puppets dancing on their miniature stage, moving up and down as the strings pull them around, following the prescribed course of their various little parts. We learn to understand the logic of this theater and we find ourselves in its motions. We locate ourselves in society and thus recognize our position as we hang from the subtle strings. For a moment we see ourselves as puppets indeed. But then we grasp a decisive difference between the puppet theater and our own drama. Unlike the puppets, we have the possibility of stopping in our movements, looking up and perceiving the machinery by which we have been moved. In this act lies the first step towards freedom. (Berger, 1963: 176)

Weaving through the book have been the thick and complementary strains of alignment and negotiation, interconnections between various social mechanisms that comprise an elaborate socio-educational landscape. Also woven through the book have been voices of individual teachers and students capturing the complex ways in which they both participate in and oppose the system. Embedded as the previous chapters are in local contexts in the Indian socio-educational scene, there appears to be at least one overall, relatively generalizable point: that issues related to the teaching and learning of English and other languages have to be understood in situated terms that account for some of the complex ways in which both oppositional and lateral forces around them operate. Searching for and understanding ways in which this system works for some people while leaving others out and as well as recognizing ways in which individuals and institutions negotiate with and within the 'system' allows us to get beyond passed-down accounts of the world 'out there' to 'see ourselves as puppets' (Berger, 1963: 176). Doing so not only stops us in our tracks and forces us to take account of strings that have moved us but to actively resist and oppose, if necessary.

The journeys entailed in this project and its writing are plural: while I address the more personal aspects in the Afterword, it is the implications and loose ends that I would like to discuss first, since some of these issues did not get the attention they deserved. As mentioned in the Preface, the English I have been writing about is Indian English, a splintered and hybrid variety that, like all languages, continues to evolve as Indian languages cast 'long shadows' (Dharwadkar 2003: 261) on it and the amalgamation and decolonization goes on. Because language policies, institutional realities, pedagogic practices, colonial legacies and postcolonial practices all mutually inform each other, they are each in themselves hybrid entitites and it is partially on this uneven, intertwined and shifting ground that my present exploration is to be understood. The overall purpose of this endeavor, for me, was to understand some dimensions of the journeys of VM students as they reach the college scene. As I have maintained throughout the book, while I was educated by the same system, it was not until I seriously began systematically searching for and piecing together parts of the canvas that I knew so little about (sheltered and insular as my associations were) that I began to have a heightened sense of how the various aspects of the system consistently aligned together to devalue Vernacular knowledges and ways of being.

Each of the previous chapters has echoed the ways in which VM students are left out of the general *assumptions nexus* that middle-class students have relatively easy access to and the generally divisive role that English seems to play in the larger scene. As we saw, the labyrinthine socio-educational system dovetails with the values and aspirations of the élite Indian middle class: not only are all tertiary-level disciplines within their reach, they also bring with them cultural models that resonate with the thought structures of EM classrooms and institutions. A range of cogs, thus, work in their favor (*our favor*; I include myself here) – national- and state-level language policies, pedagogic and institutional practices and the socio-cultural norms of their home cultures – to keep the assumptions nexus in place. Middle-class EM students can, to some extent, *assume* that the system will work for them (us) in ways that VM students cannot. The workings of the system – both at the K–12 and tertiary levels but especially at the latter – cumulatively send out direct and sometimes harsh messages regarding the generally low 'buying power' of the Vernaculars. This institutionalization of the educational system tends to 'over-pattern' the socio-educational worlds of EM and VM students to the extent of 'freezing' some of their routines, practices and choices, thereby limiting and circumscribing their behaviors. The workings of the educational system cast a veneer of a 'legitimate authority' (Wrong, 1979) on the divergent grooves and tracks on which EM and VM students progress. This kind of authority is a power relation 'in which the power holder possesses an acknowledged right to command and the power subject an acknowledged *obligation to obey*' (Wrong, 1979: 49; my emphasis). In the present case, the general socio-educational landscape is the source of power that elicits compliance from all its participants, EM and VM. The norms that make up such an authority are shared by the dominant cultural group that produces the authority in the first place, a sharing that, as we saw, produces the assumptions nexus.

Wrong (1979) points out that there is an apparent paradox in the fact that submission to legitimate authority is widely recognized as 'voluntary' and based on 'consent' rather than 'on coercion', and yet, at the same time, it is felt to be 'mandatory' or 'obligatory'. While VM students are seemingly given 'choices' in their schooling careers – whether to take English in their 10th–12th grades, for instance – the socio-educational conditions in which these 'choices' are made make one rethink the degree of true choice actually involved. As we saw, several VM students said they felt compelled to drop English after ninth grade – a 'choice' that has serious consequences in their college years. Indeed, the question to ask is perhaps: did they have a choice at all? Were they not *obliged* to drop it? There is indeed something '"mandatory" about the acceptance of authority, and no analysis can quite rationalize this mandatory element away...'(Bierstedt, cited in Wrong, 1979: 65).

While several socio-educational practices can be distilled from the complex landscape presented in these chapters, there are three that run higher risks of remaining as 'loose ends' and that demand more articulation: (1) degrees of nativization across EM and VM texts, (2) a relative focus on 'knowing your facts' (as opposed to form) and (3) the general positioning of the Vernacular in current ELTL practices. All three practices seem to have direct bearing on the procedural display in classrooms in different ways.

Nativization

While the previous chapters highlighted aspects of chasms between the VM and EM, I would like to recall a point made in the Preface and Introduction regarding all learners being at different stages of their language(s) learning journeys. Hornberger (2000) maintains that degrees of biliteracy (and nativization) exist with learners being positioned at different points along several different co-existing continua. Figure 6.1 (adapted from Hornberger & Skilton-Sylvester, 2003) lays out the different continua:

Figure 6.1 Power relations in the continua model

Traditionally less powerful	Traditionally more powerful
Context of biliteracy	
Micro	Macro
Oral	Literate
Bi(multi)lingual	Monolingual
Development of biliteracy	
Reception	Production
Oral	Written
L1	L2
Content of biliteracy	
Minority	Majority
Vernacular	Literary
Contextualized	Decontextualized
Media of biliteracy	
Simultaneous exposure	Successive exposure
Dissimilar structures	Similar structures
Divergent scripts	Convergent scripts

power, as they remind us, encompass each of the continua.

In the light of this model, degrees of nativization in VM and EM settings in the Indian context can be seen to fall at different points in each of the continua. Lest it be thought that nativization of English occurs only in VM settings and not in EM ones, I include here, as a representative sample, Kamala Das' poem (1973) about hybridization from a 10th-grade EM textbook:

An Introduction

I don't know politics but I know the names
Of those in power, and can repeat them like
Days of week or names of months, beginning with
Nehru. I am Indian, very brown, born in
Malabar, I speak three languages, write in
Two, dream in one. Don't write in English, they said.
English is not your mother-tongue. Why not leave
Me alone, critics, friends, visting cousins,
Every one of you? Why not left me speak in
Any language I like? *The language I speak
Becomes mine, its distortions, its queernesses*

All mine, mine alone. It is half English, half
Indian, funny perhaps, but it is honest.
It is human as I am human, don't
You see? It voices my joys, my longings, my
Hopes, and it is useful to me as cawing
Is to crows or roaring to the lions, it
Is human speech, the speech of the mind that is
Here and not there, a mind that sees and hears and
Is aware. Not the deaf, blind speech
Of trees in storms or of monsoon clouds of rain or the
Incoherent mutterings of the blazing
Funeral pyre. I was a child, and later they
Told me I grew.

The English used in EM settings is nativized Indian English. The fact that poems (as well as essays and stories) by Indian authors writing about local Indian scenes in an English that has long since been appropriated and 'Indianized' are included in EM textbooks at every level (K–12 and beyond) points partially to the fact that this variety is assumed to be the default.[1] However, the English used in VM textbooks (Chapter 3) may be regarded as relatively more nativized than Indian English, with more references to local scenes and more integration of local 'knowledges'. No longer does there seem to be the assumption that English (in EM or VM textbooks, settings, institutional contexts) needs to be American, British or Australian English. English in postcolonial India is Indian English.

Tugs between 'Fact' and 'Form'

One theme that resounds strongly among students and teachers in all three institutional contexts seems to be the idea that 'successful' students who 'do well in examinations' know 'their facts' (SI, 3: 6, 26). This relative emphasis on 'displaying what you know' raises an interesting nexus of issues regarding the textual politics of how students balance what they know with forms in which to display this knowledge (Ramanathan, 2003). The issue of displaying knowledge in particular ways is clearly an issue in the freshman composition industry in North America, with textbooks, pedagogic practices, curricular materials, syllabi and teacher education all working toward encouraging first- and second-language students to maintain a balance between 'form' and 'fact' in their writing. With VM and EM students in the Indian context, however, the tug between form and content/fact is less obvious for at least a couple of reasons. First, writing is not taught explicitly at the college level in anything like a 'writing course'.

Students are expected to have acquired 'composition' skills in their K–12 years, partially through the composition exercises of the sort we saw in Chapter 4. The notion of 'facts', for the private EM business college, is largely understood in disciplinary terms: whether students are able to articulate in their essays their understanding of the growth of industries in India or how national and international economic issues affect cottage industries. When asked about the significance of form in student writing, the teachers at this college had varied responses: 'Students are going to be tested on what they know and have learned, how they solve business problems, not on how they write or frame things'(FI, 15: 3); 'Many of the VM students here know their stuff, but cannot write well in English; should they be penalized for that? (FI, 17: 6); 'They should know how to write already' (FI, 16: 1). Likewise, literature teachers teaching English majors at the low-income VM college expected their students to be able to translate Chaucer and to write about Shakespeare's tragic heroines or expand on England's neoclassical age but did not seem to think that attention to the essay form at the college level when writing in English was necessary. ('The students have learned to write in Gujarati; that is enough' [FI, 8].) The EM Jesuit institution, known in the city not only to offer extra help to VM students but to also move beyond the university-mandated syllabus, also acknowledges that the general educational system privileges facts and does so partly by sustaining certain 'examination/textbook cultures'. ('There is this whole examination culture that privileges fact over form; one thing the students in our system have learned to do all through is take examinations' [FI, 6: 2].)

Sustaining the relative importance accorded to 'facts' seems to be the associated practice of gearing up for state-regulated 'Board' examinations. As we noted, teachers and students at all three institutions voiced relative urgency regarding performing successfully at these entry and exit examinations. Because these examinations typically segue into other domains of higher education and the society's social goods and because these examinations are controlled by the State Board of Education, both students and teachers, as well as classroom practices, seem oriented toward 'finishing' the syllabus in time and toward anticipating what the final examination questions might be like. This pressure to perform in these examinations, while difficult for EM students, is pronounced for their VM counterparts: as we saw, many of them feel they have little recourse but to memorize material they do not understand, especially English.

The General Positioning of the Vernacular vis-à-vis ELTL

The general institutionalization of the English–Vernacular chasm is, to a large extent, rule-governed, with rules delineating the scope and direction of individual and institutional action. The impersonality built into any socio-educational landscape – in India or elsewhere – dehumanizes it. It is against such cemented structures that efforts at critical practice and resistance need to be understood. The efforts of individual teachers and institutions to mitigate against the English–Vernacular gulf are crucial in this regard because they partially indicate that these teachers have not only taken note of the strings that manipulate their and their students' movements but take additional steps to resist the tugs actively while still participating in the performance. This delicate dance of participation and quasi-resistance shows up in a range of settings: in the ways in which teachers draw on Vernacular resources in their teaching (including resorting to them), in the ways in which they attempt to breakdown alien, western concepts into local, accessible terms, in the ways in which they militate to have Indian writing in English included in university syllabi, in making opportunities for VM and EM students to participate in extra-curricular events, in making time and room for extra courses for VM students (with no recompense) so that these students can also compete in the larger system. We saw teachers at all three institutions using the Vernacular in different ways. At the women's college, we saw teachers engage in critical practices by drawing on the Vernacular in a variety of ways, using it as their medium of instruction, as well as by drawing on its folklore and traditional uses so that they could bridge gulfs between students' home cultures and the unfamiliar content of their students' English literature textbooks. We also noted that teachers at this institution recognize the largely pro-English/anti-Vernacular tendencies of the larger system and work to resist the pressure to become overly pro-English themselves; i.e. by ensuring that they hired faculty who could teach in the Vernacular and by finding non-academic ways of building up the self-esteem of their VM students. In a similar vein, teachers at the business college do not hesitate to use the Vernacular outside the classroom to help their students, just as the VM coordinator does not hesitate to admit more eligible VM students, despite the disgruntlement of his colleagues. The Jesuit institution, too, has found varying ways to bridge the English–Vernacular chasm: in the ways in which it integrates the Vernaculars in everyday interactions with students, in the extensive reverse translating that teachers engage in as a way of ensuring comprehension in both Gujarati and English, in recognizing that the teaching of English literature is not going to meet the language needs of their VM students (and their subsequent lobbying for and acquiring a new Communicative English course). Although the larger socio-educational system at all three colleges – and other tertiary level institutions – tends to devalue Vernaculars and their associated practices, there are clearly small but significant ways in which the English–Vernacular chasm is critically countered. Exploring and addressing such efforts

provides for the possibility that, in everyday life, the powerless in post-colonial communities may find ways to negotiate, alter, and oppose political structures, and reconstruct their languages, cultures, and identities to their advantage. The intention is not to reject English, but to reconstitute it in more inclusive, ethical and democratic terms. (Canagarajah, 1999a: 2)

The efforts at mitigating the English–Vernacular gulf as charted in this book are primarily those of teachers and institutions whose explicit aim is to empower VM students by both validating their students' (Vernacular) backgrounds and by reconstituting ELTL in more 'inclusive, ethical and democratic terms' (as specified in the previous quote) so as to ultimately counter dominant alignments. Students educated in the Vernacular typically arrive at the EM college scene having been socialized into models of English literacy that are 'less powerful' (socially, culturally, politically, economically) than their EM counterparts. (Indeed, the procedural display that we saw in the women's and business colleges can be seen to be set in place long before the VM students make it to college, after which these students are slotted into state-legitimized tracks.) Efforts that the Jesuit institution and the individual teachers make are, in Canagarajah's terms, efforts at negotiating, altering and opposing political structures.

While it is easy for those of us on the sidelines to suggest changes – heightening awareness that language and literature teaching are entirely separate endeavors, that Vernacular and English language learning and teaching practices should not be pitted in dichotomous terms, that the English language and literature course syllabi needs serious revision, that VM students need to have equal access to a tertiary-level education that more closely resonates with what they bring with them – realities on the ground are immensely complex. Equally complex has been the writing process of this manuscript. Caught between several competing discourses, positions and intentions, any general sense of coherence that emerges from this text is a manufactured one: not only are realities on the ground are far too intertwined and overlapping for any discursive act to do justice but my own positioning vis-à-vis VM students, as an EM product, is multifaceted as well. As mentioned in the Introduction, an aim of this exploration was not to advocate any one stance or solution, on either Vernacular or English teaching, as much as it was to arrive at a nuanced, fine-grained, multidimensional canvas of how entrenched English and the Vernaculars are in language policies and practices, procedural displays, peripheral worlds of students and teachers, political orientations of institutions and the dedication of individual teachers and institutions. What emerges as socio-educational practices – memorizing, using study guides, eliciting choral responses, emphasizing 'correct' answers – is really a mixture of several co-occurring factors, including drawing on Vernacular and home traditions, latent ideological currents, socialization practices in schools and transmitted cultural models in particular pedagogical tools. Aspects of these various cogs are highlighted, produced and resisted in certain domains, in certain contexts and institutions over others and, while we may single some of them out for closer inspection, we cannot lose sight of the larger landscape of which they are apart. English's divisive role in this context needs to be understood against this most complex scene (Dua, 2001).

The interpretive (native) 'researcher', then, is left with the question of how to arrive at a methodology that best captures these complexly intertwined strands. Such complexities force the 'researcher' to explore the 'data' from many different angles toward achieving a more fine-grained picture of both social inequalities as well as areas of possible and currently practiced avenues of social change. Because contact zones are, by their very nature, very complex spaces that house dominations and resistances and chasms and bridges, 'the challenge is to understand these relationships [between the numerous and intertwined cogs] and to find ways of always focusing on the local while at the same time keeping an eye on the broader horizons' (Pennycook, 2000: 102). The book ends, then, with perhaps more and different questions than those with which it began: In what ways is English simultaneously divisive and integrated on the postcolonial ground and what local forms does this take? Can we as committed teachers, scholars and students find critical ways to ensure that the Vernaculars (and the numerous students raised, socialized and educated in them) are not devalued? And finally, can we, as researchers, find ways of addressing both social stratifications and local resistances, of exploring discursive methods that capture the fluid, hybrid, overlapping nature of all learning and teaching, while also being mindful of chasms and gulfs?

Note

1.   Indian English is its own English: it is only outside India that it is seen as a 'variety'.

Afterword: Some Personal Notes

Because this exploration is a journey (several journeys, actually) into aspects of the educational world that raised and schooled me, I feel doubly obliged to acknowledge openly and share the ways in which this project has made me confront very many corners of myself that I kept hidden. While I was intellectually aware that class and caste are divisive issues, it was not until this exploration got underway that I realized the extent to which my class and caste status in my 'home' culture afforded me access to the assumptions nexus that I had so completely assumed as my 'birthright': access to the privileged world of 'good' schools, extra-curricular activities, books and a lifestyle that is best captured by that catch-all, over-used, phrase 'middle class'. I found myself growing self-conscious of what and how much I really had and was (and still am) on several occasions embarrassed and even ashamed of what my privileged status indexes. When going to the inner-city women's college, I found myself hating some of the middle-class totings of my person – my short, westernized haircut, my leather handbag and shoes (despite my Indian garb) – and found myself looking for ways to blend in. Spending countless hours talking to, listening, reading and thinking about caste issues made me very sharply aware of how different the socio-educational landscape seems to someone 'lower' on the 'caste scale', how institutionalized 'labels' (such as 'Schedule Castes', and 'Other Backward Classes') and tracking policies for fellow Indians work to create, legitimize and reinforce unequal grooves. My vision of the world had been utterly and embarrassingly myopic.

As if these painful realizations were not enough, there are at least two others that stare me in the face everyday: as one directly engaged in English-language teacher education, I worry that I am contributing to sustaining the divisive force that English plays in the world. The only way in which I make my peace with this difficult predicament is by working to make my second-language student-teachers more critical, more vigilant and more reflective of their practices so that they can think of ways of changing aspects of their (TESOL-related) socio-educational worlds. Knowing what I do now about the challenges VM students and teachers face, doing TESOL as usual is no longer possible. While I have had students and colleagues argue with me saying that India and the Anglo-phone world are totally different social realities, that the English-related gulfs in India have little bearing on the TESOL agenda of western countries, I am also keenly aware, like some of my other colleagues, that the ever-hastening globalization process is connecting landscapes in faster, intrusive ways and that socio-educational realties in other 'very different' parts of the world have a direct bearing on realms such as teacher education in the western world. The other painful issue is the one with which I began this book and that I mention in the preface: the politics of representation. Am I assuming the right to speak for VM students, and to what extent do my caste, class and EM background give me that 'right'? I could of course, have chosen not to write on this project: the issues and my own positioning in relation to them can be seen as questionable. But can I now, understanding what I do of some of the unequal realities on the ground, really be quiet?

Appendix 1: Details of Research Data

The three institutions were:

    (a) an EM Jesuit college,
    (b) a VM women's college and
    (c) a private, EM business college.

Data from the Three Institutions

Written documents:

These comprised:

- university–mandated syllabi across several disciplines,
- brochures (advertising particular programs, especially from PCC),
- university exam questions of previous years,
- memos/notices,
- textbooks (K-12, and college-level) and
- student essays, notes, study props and guides, grammar work-books.

Classroom observations and field notes

EM Jesuit college	*VM women's college*	*EM private business college*
Total number of Faculty interviewed: 9	Total number of faculty interviewed: 6	Total number of faculty interviewed: 6
Observations of class in English Compulsory (15 hours), Literature classes (5 hours), 'Bridge courses' (5 hours) Psychology (3 hours), Economics (2 hours), Gujarati literature (3 hours) **Total**: 33 hours	Observations of classes in: English Language (21 hours), Literature (7 hours), Economics (3 hours), Sanskrit (4 hours), Hindi,(2 hours) and Gujarati (3 hours) and Psychology (2 hours) **Total**: 42 hours	Observation of classes in: Accounting (6 hours), Growth of Industries (8 hours), Economics (7 hours) and Commercial Communication (13 hours) **Total**: 34 hours
Field notes: canteen, hall-ways, faculty office, basketball/football courts	Field notes: parking structure, hallways, outside faculty offices	Field notes: cafeterias, library, campus grounds, hallways, parking lots, faculty offices

Interview themes

Partial list for students at all three schools:

their English language backgrounds (when they began learning English),
why they chose the institution they did,
what they would like to see get out of their degree,
their future plans: graduate school, jobs, marriage,
parental pressure,
their majors and why they chose them,
experiences learning English in school,
the general importance they accord to English,
what they think works in the current educational system and what does not,
what they would like to see changed in institutional and state-wide policies,
how they prepare for exams,
areas of encouragement (regarding their schooling) in their lives,
level of difficulty in college-level English as compared to school,
how they deal with essay exams,
problems with writing,
issues in writing extensively,
what they would like to see changed about English instruction.

Partial list for teachers/administrators at all three schools:

years of service at the institution,
subjects they teach,
some of their most rewarding moments in their teaching,
areas in the school/university they think need change; where writing practices fit in,
how these problems can be addressed,
biggest challenges facing Gujarati-medium students,
challenges facing female students,
their definition of a 'good student',
the role of exams,
their views about K–12 in the city schools,
their views on university prescribed textbooks,
particular problems faced by VM English literature students,
particular problems faced by all a- and b-stream VM students; problems related to tracking,

class-related, socio-cultural conventions that they think their students follow,

number of students that use English outside class,

what they do to make texts accessible to students,

problems with the exam system, student responses, writing problems,

how the institution compares with others in the state,

their general philosophy regarding teaching,

the kinds of academic, career-related expectations students bring with them,

what they would like to see changed: in the larger system, in classroom, in the institution they work for.

Appendix 2: Some Historical Dates Marking the Enforcement of Particular Educational Policies

This was drawn from Chatterjee, 1992.

1823: *Appointment of Committee of Public Instruction* in Bengal. Raja Ram Mohan Roy requests Lord Amherst – then Governor-General – to establish a 'liberal and enlightened system of instruction embracing natural philosophy' instead of the proposed Sanskrit college in Calcutta (Chatterjee, 1992: 300).

1835: *Macaulay's Minute* that led to institutionalizing English education.

1854: *Wood's Despatch*. Charles Wood moves to establish a department of education that governs the establishment of universities in Presidency towns. 'This results in selective higher education for training future administrators, imparted through the medium of English, and in 'useful and practical' education for the rest of society, imparted through the vernaculars, thus confirming indigenous patterns of social stratification' (Chatterjee, 1992: 300).

1857–87: *Establishment of universities* in Calcutta, Bombay, Madras, Lahore and Allahabad.

1882: *Indian Education Commission*. Established to monitor progress of education. In its Report (1884), the Commission recommends improving primary and elementary education and confirms university policy. Social stratification widens.

1904: *Indian Universities Act*. The Viceroy, Lord Curzon, tightens government control over university and college administration and provides funds for setting up laboratories and museums.

1948–49: *University Education Commission*. This deals specifically with issues related to the medium of education. 'English was not considered desirable for these reasons: (1) it is a negation of democracy since it divides the Indian people into two nations: the few who govern, and the many who are governed; and (2) it is educationally unsound to use a foreign language. Hindi is recommended as the medium of instruction, the Devanagri script to be reformed and used for this purpose. The study of English to continue' (Chatterjee, 1992: 302).

1961: *Three language formula*. This sets in motion the study of the following three languages in schools: (1) regional language or mother tongue, (2) Hindi or any other Indian language in Hindi-speaking areas, and (3) English or any other European language. Not adopted across the board.

1964–66: *Education Commission Report.* This was set up under Dr D.S. Kothari.

Recognizes the language question as one of the most complex and intractable of India's post-Independence problems... Recommends the use of regional languages as media of instruction...recommends both Hindi and English as link languages, while recognizing that English cannot serve as link for the majority. Confirms Three-Language Formula and recommends the third language be studied from the point of view of national integration.

Use of English to continue as library language...no student to be considered as qualified for a degree unless she has acquired a reasonable proficiency in English; all teachers consequently to be bilingual.

Recommends special units to be set up for teaching English as a language skill, as distinct from teaching as literature. English to be the medium of instruction in all major universities because of their all-India character. (Chatterjee, 1992: 303)

1967: *Official Languages Amendment Bill.* 'Seeks to give statutory recognition to Jawaharlal Nehru's assurance regarding the continued use of English as long as non-Hindi speaking people do not desire a change'. (Chatterjee, 2002: 304)

1968: *National Policy on Education.* This draws on the Kothari Commission. 'Emphasis on the need to inculcate democratic values and national integration. Uniformity in courses of study, evaluation procedures and number of years to be spent at each stage of the educational process ought' (Chatterjee, 1992: 304).

1989: *Angrezi Hatao* (Remove English) Movement in Uttar Pradesh. Punjab militants insist on the use of Punjabi in all official transactions and in the media. Echoes language riots in Tamilnadu against the use of Hindi.

Appendix 3: Divergent Minimal Levels of Learning (MLLs) for VM and EM Students

	Excerpts from MLL from English textbooks used in the Gujarati-medium	Excerpts from MLLs from English textbooks used in the English-medium
Grade 5	*Writing:* Gain control of the basic mechanics of writing in English like capital letters, small letters, punctuation, writing neatly on a line with proper spacing Transcribe words, phrases and sentences in English Write cardinals up to fifty, telephone numbers, road signs Produces words and spells them correctly Write numbers up to fifty, telephone numbers, road signs	*Reading and writing:* Reading textual material and writing answers to questions based on and related to the text Reading and interpreting and offering comments on maps and charts Reading children's literature and talking about it Writing paragraphs on given topics Reading and writing simple recipes Reading and interpreting labels on wrappers
Grade 6	*Reading: Reads aloud simple sentences, poems, dialogues and short passages with proper pauses* *Reads and follows given directions* *Reads numbers upto a hundred* *Writing:* Writes with proper punctuation marks Writes words and sentences neatly on a line with proper spacing, punctuation marks, and capitalization Writes answers to questions based on text material Writes simple guided compositions in 4–5 sentences on people, objects, or places Translates words and sentences from English into Gujarati and Gujarati into English	*Reading and writing:* Reading textual material and writing answers to questions based on the text Reading and interpreting simple abbreviations Reading narrative prose and adventure stories and talking about them Writing/building stories based on given questions/points Reading and using the telephone directory Writing captions for given photographs, pictures, maps, charts, diagrams and graphs Writing messages for telegrams Reading and interpreting labels on bottles
Grade 7	*Reading: Reads aloud simple sentences* *Finds key words and phrases from a text* *Writing:* Writes words and sentences and paragraphs dictated with correct spellings, proper punctuation marks Learns to write words and sentences neatly on a line with proper spacing and punctuation Writes answers to questions based on the text Writes simple guided compositions Writes informal chits [notes] – thank-you notes and invitations (Purani *et al.*, 1998: 1–3)	*Reading and writing:* Reading textual material and writing answers based on the text Writing essays based on the text Reading literary stories and prose lessons Reading simple passages of reflective prose Reading and interpreting common instructions such as railway timetables Reading and interpreting maps, labels Reading short plays/passages/writing summaries (Purani *et al.*, 1998: 2)

Appendix 4: Examples from Curricula and Examination Papers

Paper 3 – from the History of English Literature 1798–1900

(From The Second-Year English Literature Syllabus, Gujarat University Curriculum, 2000–2001: 15–16)

(1) Two *essay questions* on the following topics can be asked. Questions could be asked on a particular author or authors under a particular topic:

Romantic revival and its chief characteristics
The personal essay
The Victorian compromise
Trends in Victorian poetry
The novel in the 19th century
Victorian prose writers
Pre-Raphaelite poetry

(2) One question will test students' acquaintance with the works of writers of the period. The following will be studied. Seven titles will be asked. Students, *in essays*, will write the name of the author, the date of publication, and the type of work and relate it to the period.

Poetry	*Novels*	*Essays*
Lyrical Ballads	Pride and Prejudice	Table Talk
The Prelude	Vanity Fair	Imaginary Conversation
Adonais	A Tale of Two Cities	Sarter Resartus
Idylls of the king	The Mill on the Floss	Unto This Last
Sohrab and Rustum	Wuthering Heights	Essays in Criticism
Atlanta in Calydon	Barchester Towers	The Confessions of an
The Rime of the Ancient	The return of the Native	english Opium Eater
mariner	The Egoist	On Heroes and Hero
	David Copperfield	worship
	The Cloister and the	Modern Painters
	hearth	

Sample exam in Commercial English

(1) The play 'The Pillars of Society' tries to expose the lies, corruption, and hypocrisy prevailing in the society and the fear of public opinion. Discuss.

(2) Write a press report on any one:
- An air crash
- A severe earthquake causing damage to life and property
- A vote of confidence and the fall of a government

(3) A committee has been appointed by Adarsh Associates Ltd. to look into the grievances of the workers of the company. Prepare the committee's report.
OR
As the General Manager of a Joint Stock Company, prepare a report on the working of the branch offices of the company situated in the state of Gujarat.

(4) Write an essay on any one:
(a) Political uncertainty
(b) Computers and human life
(c) Importance of education in business. (From Desai & Patel, 2000: 327–8)

Bridge course for first-year, b-stream students (21 lectures, 45 minutes each)

Components

(1) The use of the dictionary (letters of the alphabet and alphabetical order)
(2) Parts of speech
(3) Articles
(4) Person: first, second, third
(5) Verbs
(6) Number: singular, plural
(7) Auxiliaries
(8) Types of sentences: assertive, negative, interrogative, imperative, exclamatory. (From The English Compulsory Syllabus for the First Year, Gujarat University Curriculum, 2000: 22)

Structure of the second-year English Compulsory exam

Test section	Task	Marks assigned
Short notes	Write a paragraph on a specific term, concept, or character	10
Short-answer questions	Write a paragraph in response to a question	10
Advertisements	Answer questions based on advertise-ments (e.g. jobs available, products for sale)	5
Short news items	Interpret excerpts from newspapers or other general news sources	5
Reading passage	Note the main points	5
Letter writing	Write a job application letter or a letter to a friend	7
Pronunciation	Identify which syllable in a list of words is stressed	10
Word building	In Scrabble-like games, create a certain number of words from an assortment of letters	10
One-word substitutes	Choose one of four phrases that best repre-sents the meaning of a word	7

References

Adam, I. and. Tiffin, H. (eds) (1991) *Past The Last Post: Theorizing Postcolonialism and Postmodernism.* Calgary: University of Calgary Press.

Agarwal, J. C. (1984) *Landmarks in the History of Modern Indian Education.* New Delhi: Vikas.

Ageira, B. (1996) *Crisis in Primary Education.* Agra: Y.K. Publishers.

Ager, D. (2001) *Motivation in Language Planning and Language Policy.* Clevedon: Multilingual Matters.

Albrecht, C. (2002) An ecological and Jesuit calling. *Promotio Iustitiae,* p. 5–7.

Anyon, J. (1997) *Ghetto Schooling: A Political Economy of Urban Educational Reform.* New York: Teacher's College Press.

Appadurai, A. (1988) Introduction: Place and voice in anthropological theory. *Cultural Anthropology* 3(1), 16–20.

Apple, M. (1990) *Ideology and Curriculum.* New York: Routledge.

Apple, M. and Christian-Smith, L. (ed.) (1991) *The Politics of the Textbook.* New York: Routledge.

Atkinson, D. (2001) Reflections and refractions of the JSLW special issue on voice. *Journal of Second Language Writing* 10(1, 2), 107–24.

Atkinson, D. and Ramanathan, V. (1995) 'Cultures of writing': An ethnographic comparison of L1 and L2 university writing/language programs. *TESOL Quarterly* 29(3), 539–68.

Atkinson, P. (1992) *Understanding Ethnographic Texts.* Newbury Park, CA: Sage.

Baker, C. (1988) *Key Issues in Bilingualism and Bilingual Education.* Clevedon: Multilingual Matters.

Baker, C. (2000) *The Care and Education of Young Bilinguals.* Clevedon: Multilingual Matters.

Baker, C. (2003) Biliteracy and transliteracy in Wales: Language planning and the Welsh national curriculum. In Nancy Hornberger (ed.) *Continua of Biliteracy: An Ecological Framework for Educational Policy, Research, and Practice in Multilingual Settings* (pp. 71–90). Clevedon: Multilingual Matters.

Bauldauf, R. and Luke, A. (1990) (eds.) *Language Planning and Education in Australasia and the South Pacific.* Clevedon: Multilingual Matters.

Berger, P. (1963) *Invitation to Sociology: A Humanistic Perspective.* New York: Anchor Press.

Berger, P. and Luckmann, T. (1966) *The Social Construction of Reality: A Treatise on the Sociology of Knowledge.* Garden City, NY: Doubleday.

Berger, P. and Luckmann, T. (1967) *The Social Construction of Reality.* Garden City, NY: Doubleday.

Bhattacharya, S. (ed.) (1998) *The Contested Terrain: Perspectives on Education in India* (pp. 3–26). New Delhi: Orient Longman.

Bloch, C. and Alexander, N. (2003) A Luta Continua!: The relevance of the continua of biliteracy to South African multilingual schools. In Nancy Hornberger (ed.) *Continua of Biliteracy: An Ecological Framework for Educational Policy, Research, and*

Practice in Multilingual Settings (pp. 91–121). Clevedon: Multilingual Matters.

Bloome, D., Puro, P. and Theodoru, E. (1989) Procedural display and classroom lessons. *Curriculum Inquiry* 19(3), 265–91.

Bruthiaux, P. (2002) Hold your courses: Language education, language choice, and economic development. *TESOL Quarterly* 36(3), 275–96.

Canagarajah, S. (1999a) *Resisting Imperialism in English Teaching*. Oxford: Oxford University Press.

Canagarajah, S. (1999b) Of EFL teachers, awareness, and agency. *ELT Journal* 53(3), 207–16.

Candlin, C. and Mercer, N. (2001) *Teaching English in its Social Context*. London: Routledge.

Chakrabarty, D. (2000) *Provincializing Europe*. Princeton, NJ: Princeton University Press.

Chatterjee, L. (1992) Landmarks in official educational policy: Some facts and figures. In R.S Rajan (ed.) *The Lie of the Land* (pp. 300–308). New Delhi: Oxford University Press.

Clifford, J. (1990) Notes on (field)notes. In R. Sanjek (ed.) *Fieldnotes: The Makings of Anthropology*. Ithaca, NY: Cornell University Press.

Crismore, A. (1984) The rhetoric of the textbook: Metadiscourse. *Curriculum Studies* 16 (3), 279–96.

Crismore, A. (1988) *The Interaction of Metadiscourse and Anxiety in Determining Children's Learning of Social Studies Textbook Materials* (pp. 1–24). Washington, DC: Center for the Study of Reading, University of Illinois.

Crook, N. (ed.) (1996) *The Transmission of Knowledge in South Asia*. Delhi: Oxford University Press.

Cummins, J. (2000) *Language, Power, and Pedagogy: Bilingual Children in the Crossfire*. Clevedon: Multilingual Matters.

Cummins, J. (2001) *Negotiating Identities: Education for Empowerment in a Diverse Society*. Los Angeles, CA: California Association for Bilingual Education.

Cummins, J. and Skutnabb-Kangas, T. (eds) (1988) *Minority Education: From Shame to Struggle*. Clevedon: Multilingual Matters.

D'Andrade, R. (1990) Cultural cognition. In M. L. Posner (ed.) *Foundations of Cognitive Science* (pp. 795–830). Cambridge, MA: MIT Press.

Das, K. (1973) A poem: An introduction. In *The Old Play House and Other Stories*. Madras: Orient Longman.

Desai, S.D. and Patel, A.L. (1999) *Modern Commercial Communication*. Ahmedabad: C. Jamnadas and Co.

Dharwadkar, V. (2003) The historical formation of Indian English literature. In Sheldon Pollock (ed.) *Literary Cultures in History: Reconstructions from South Asia* (pp. 199–267). Berkeley, CA: University of California Press.

Dirks, N. (2001) *Castes of Mind*. Princeton: Princeton University Press.

D'souza, T. (1994) Education and mission: The school as agent of evangelization in India. In T. D'souza (ed.) *Discoveries, Missionary Expansion, and Asian Cultures* (pp. 58–75). New Delhi: Concept.

Dua, H. (1994) *The Hegemony of English*. Jaipur: Yashoda.

Dua, H. (2001) *Science Policy Education and Language Planning*. Mysore: Yashoda.

Eagleton, T. (1991) *Ideology: An Introduction*. London: Verson.

Fleck, L. (1981) *Genesis and the Development of a Scientific Fact*. Chicago: Chicago University Press.

Foucault, P. (1972) *The Archeology of Knowledge.* London: Tavistock Publications.
Foucault, P. (1978) *The History of Sexuality.* New York: Pantheon.
Gandhi, L. (1998) *Postcolonial Theory.* New York: Colombia University Press.
Gandhi, M.K. (1954) *Medium of Instruction.* (B. Kumarappa, Trans.) Ahmedabad: Navjivan.
Gargesh, R. (1995) Comments on the eighth schedule languages: A critical perspective. In R. Gupta, A. Abbi and K. Agarwal (eds) *Language and the State: Perspectives on the Eighth Schedule* (pp. 87–91). New Delhi: Creative Books.
Gee, J. (1990) *Social Linguistics and Literacies: Ideologies in Discourses.* Bristol, PA: Falmer Press.
Gee, J. (1999) *An Introduction to Discourse Analysis: Theory and Method.* London: Routledge.
Gramsci, A. (1988) *A Gramsci Reader: Selected Writings.* London: Lawrence Wishart.
Greene, J. and Bloome, D. (1997) Ethnography and ethnographers of and in education: A situated perspective. In J. Flood, S. B. Heath and D. Lappe (eds) *Handbook of Research on Teaching Literacy Through the Communicative and Visual Arts* (pp. 181–201). New York: Simon and Schuster, Macmillan.
Goodwin, J. (2001) Teaching pronunciation. In M. Celce-Murcia (ed.) *Teaching English as a Second or Foreign Language* (pp. 117–133). Boston: Heinle and Heinle.
Guha, R. (1997) *Dominance without Hegemony: History and Power in Colonial India.* Cambridge, MA: Harvard University Press.
Gujarat State Board of School Textbooks (1999) *Mininum Levels of Learning* (pp. 1–2). Gandhinagar: Gujarat State Board of School Textbooks.
Gupta, R., Abbi, A. and Agarwal, K. (eds) (1995) *Language and the State: Perspectives on the Eighth Schedule.* New Delhi: Creative Books.
Hasnain, I. (1995) Comments on the eighth schedule: A linguistic perspective. In R. Gupta, A. Ami and K. Agarwal (eds) *Language and the State: Perspectives on the Eighth Schedule* (pp. 59–60). New Delhi: Creative Books.
Heredia, R. (2000) Persistence and crisis in Indian Education. *Social Action* 50, 364–371.
Hirvela, A. and Belcher, D. (2001) Coming back to voice: The multiple voices and identities of mature multilingual writers. *Journal of Second Language Writing* 10, 81–106.
Holliday, A. (1994) *Appropriate Methodology and Social Context.* Cambridge: Cambridge University Press.
Hornberger, N. (1995) Five vowels or three? Linguistics and politics in Quechua language planning in Peru. In James Tollefson (ed.) *Power and Inequality in Language Education* (pp.187–205). Cambridge: Cambridge University Press.
Hornberger, N. (2000) Multilingual literacies, literacy practices, and the continua of biliteracy. In Marilyn Martin-Jones and Kathryn Jones (eds) *Multilingual Literacies.* (pp. 353–357). Philadelphia: John Benjamins.
Hornberger, N. (ed.) (2003) *Continua of Biliteracy: An Ecological Framework for Educational Policy, Research, and Practice in Multilingual Settings.* Clevedon: Multilingual Matters.
Hornberger, N. and Skilton-Sylvester, E. (2003) Revisiting the continua of biliteracy: International and critical perspectives. In Nancy Hornberger (ed.) *Continua of Biliteracy: An Ecological Framework for Educational Policy, Research, and Practice in Multilingual Settings* (pp. 35–67). Clevedon: Multilingual Matters.
Jadeja, R., Shrinivas, R. and Vansia, K. (1999) *English, Standard 5.* Gandhinagar: Gujarat State Board of Textbooks.

Jawaare, A. (1998) The silence of the subaltern student. In S. Tharu (ed.) *Subject to Change* (pp. 1–32). Hyderabad: Orient Longman.

Jayaram, N. (1993) The language question in higher education: Trends and issues. In Suma Chitnis and Phillip Albach (eds) *Higher Education Reform in India* (pp. 84–119) New Delhi: Sage.

Kachru, Braj (1997) World Englishes 2000: Resources for research and teaching. In Larry Smith and Michael Forman (eds) *World English 2000* (pp. 209–51). Honolulu: University of Hawaii Press.

Kamble, N. (1983) *Deprived Castes and Their Struggle for Equality*. New Delhi: Ashish.

Khan, J., Desai, R. and Vyas, H. (eds) (2000) *English, Standard 12*. Gandhinagar: Gujarat State Board of Textbooks.

Khilnani, S. (1998) *The Idea of India*. New Delhi: Penguin.

Khubchandani, L. (1995) The eighth schedule as a device for language engineering. In R. Gupta, A. Ami and K. Agarwal (eds) *Language and the State: Perpectives on the Eighth Schedule* (pp. 30–41). New Delhi: Creative Books.

Kotak, G., Ghodiwala, A., Purani, T. and Pandya, N. (1996) *English Reader: Standard 8*. Gandhinagar: Gujarat State Board of Textbooks.

Kotak, G., Ghodiwala, A., Purani, T. and Pandya, N. (1999) *English Reader: Standard 5*. Gandhinagar: Gujarat State Board of Textbooks.

Kotak, G., Jadeja, R. and Joshi, P. (1998) *English Reader: Standard 10*. Gandhinagar: Gujarat State Board of Textbooks.

Kumar, K. (1987) Origins of India's 'textbook culture'. *Occasional Papers on History and Society* XLVII, 1–32.

Latour, B. (1996) *Laboratory Life: The Construction of Scientific Facts*. Princeton, NJ: Princeton University Press.

Loomba, A. (1998) Teaching the bard in India. In S. Tharu (ed.) *Subject to Change* (pp. 33–51). Hyderabad: Orient Longman.

MacIntyre, A. (1985) *After Virtue*. London: Duckworth.

Martin-Jones, M. and Jones, K. (2000) *Multilingual Literacies*. Philadelphia: John Benjamins.

Matsuda, P. (2001) Voice in Japanese written discourse: Implications for second language writing. *Journal of Second Language Writing* 10, 35–53.

May, S. (2001) *Language and Minority Rights: Ethnicity, Nationalism, and the Politics of Language*. London: Longman.

Mercado, C. (2003) Biliteracy development among Latino youth in New York city communities: An unexploited potential. In Nancy Hornberger (ed.) *Continua of Biliteracy: An Ecological Framework for Educational Policy, Research, and Practice in Multilingual Settings*. Clevedon: Multilingual Matters.

Ministry of Education, (1968) *National Policy on Education* (pp. 1–10). New Delhi: Government of India

Moses, D., Soni, P., Jadeja, R. and Kapadia, S. (ed.) (2000) *English: Standard 11*. Gandhinagar: Gujarat State Board of Textbooks.

Mwijage, P. (2002) Historical origins of our Jesuit committment to Justice. *Promotio Iustitiae*, 1–4.

Naregal, V. (2001) *Language, Politics, Elites, and Public Sphere: Western India Under Colonialism*. New Delhi: Orient Longman.

Nataraj, S. and. Joshi, P. (1999) *English: Standard 5*. Gandhinagar: Gujarat State Board of Textbooks.

Nataraj, S., Joshi, P. and Pandya, N. (1998) *English Reader: Standard 6*. Gandhinagar: Gujarat State Board of Textbooks.

Nunan, D. (ed.) (1992) *Collaborative Language Learning and Teaching*. Cambridge: Cambridge University Press.

Pal, A., Nagar, A. and Chakraborty, T. (2001) *Decolonization: A Search for Alternatives*. New Delhi: Creative Books.

Pannikar, K.N. (1998) *Culture, Ideology, and Hegemony: Intellectuals and Social Consciousness in Colonial India*. New Delhi: Tulika.

Pattanayak, D.P. (1981) *Multilingualism and Mother-tongue Education*. Bombay: Oxford University Press.

Pattanayak, D.P. (ed.) (1990) *Multilingualism in India*. Clevedon: Multilingual Matters.

Pechey, G. (1994) Post-apartheid narratives. In F. Baker, P. Hulme and M. Iversen (eds) *Colonial Discourse/Postcolonial Theory* (pp. 151–71). New York: Manchester University Press.

Pennycook, A. (1996) English, universities, and struggles over culture and knowledge. In Ruth Hayhoe and Julia Pan (eds) *East–West Dialogue in Knowledge and Higher Education* (pp. 64–80). London: M.E. Sharpe.

Pennycook, A. (1998) *English and the Discourses of Colonialism*. London: Routledge.

Pennycook, A. (2000) The social politics and the cultural politics of language classrooms. In Joan Kelly Hall and William Eggington (eds) *The Sociopolitics of English Language Teaching* (pp. 89–103). Clevedon: Multilingual Matters.

Phillipson, R. (1992) *Linguistic Imperialism*. Oxford: Oxford University Press.

Prior, P. (2001) Voices in text, mind, and society. *Journal of Second Language Writing* 10, 55–81.

Purani, T., Nityanandanan, I. and Patel, S. (1998) *English Reader: Standard 6*. Gandhinagar: Gujarat State Board of Textbooks.

Purani, T., Nityanandanan, I. and Vansia, K. (1999) *English: Standard 7*. Gandhinagar: Gujarat State Board of Textbooks.

Quigley, D. (1993) *The Interpretation of Caste*. New York: Clarendon Press.

Rajan, R.S. (1986) 'After Orientalism': Colonialism and English literary studies in India. *Social Scientist* 158, 23–35.

Rajan, S.R. (1992) *The Lie of the Land*. Delhi: Oxford University Press.

Rajagopalan, K. (1999) Of EFL teachers, conscience, and cowardice. *ELT Journal* 53, 200–06.

Ramanathan, S. (2002) On the teaching of literature to *a* and *b* stream students. (Personal communication). Ahmedabad, 8 November

Ramanathan, V. (1999) 'English is here to stay': A critical look at institutional and educational practices in India. *TESOL Quarterly* 33(2), 211–31.

Ramanathan, V. (2002a) *The Politics of TESOL Education: Writing, Knowledge, Critical Pedagogy*. New York: Routledge Falmer.

Ramanathan, V. (2002b) What does 'literate in English' mean? A critical examination of divergent literacy practices for vernacular vs. English-medium students in India. *Canadian Modern Language Review* 59(3), 125–51.

Ramanathan,V. (2003) Written textual production and consumption (WTPC) in vernacular and English-medium settings in Gujarat, India. *Journal of Second Language Writing* 12(2), 125–50.

Ramanathan, V. and Atkinson, D. (1999) Individualism, academic writing and ESL writers. *Journal of Second Language Writing* 8(1), 45–75.

Ramanathan, V., Davies, C. and Schleppegrell, M. (2001) A naturalistic inquiry into the cultures of two MA-TESOL programs: Implications for TESOL. *TESOL Quarterly* 35(2), 279–305.

Raval, H. and Nakum, G. (1996) *A Textbook of English Language Teaching*. Ahmedabad: B.S. Shah Prakashan.

Ricento, T. (2000) Introduction. In T. Ricento (ed.) *Ideology, Politics and Language Policies* (pp. 1–24). Philadelphia: John Benjamins.

Rouse, J. (1994) Power/knowledge. In Gary Gutting (ed.) *The Cambridge Companion to Foucault*. Cambridge, UK: Cambridge University Press.

Sanjek, R. (ed.) (1990) *Fieldnotes: The Makings of Anthropology*. Ithaca, NY: Cornell University Press.

Sarkar, J. (1984) *Caste, Occupation, and Change*. Delhi: B. R. Publishing.

Shuman, J. (1985) *Keeping Track*. New Haven, CT: Yale University Press.

Schiffman, H. (1996) *Linguistic Culture and Language Policy*. London: Routledge.

Shore, B. (1996) *Culture in Mind*. Oxford: Oxford University Press.

Simon, R. (1992) *Teaching Against the Grain*. New York: Bergin &Garvey.

Singh, R.P. (1998) British educational policy in 19th century India: A nationalist critique. In S. Bhattacharya (ed.) *The Contested Terrain: Perspectives on Education in India* (pp. 99–121). New Delhi: Sage.

Skutnabb-Kangas, T. and Phillipson, R. (eds) (1995) *Linguistic Human Rights: Overcoming Linguistic Discrimination*. Berlin: Mouton de Gruyter.

Smith, Larry and Forman, Michael (eds) (1997) *World Englishes 2000*. Honolulu, Hawaii: University of Hawaii Press.

Spolsky, B. (ed.) (1986) *Language and Education in Multilingual Settings*. Clevedon: Multilingual Matters.

Spurr, D. (1993) *The Rhetoric of Empire: Colonial Discourse in Journalism, Travel Writing, and Imperial Administration*. Durham, NC: Duke University Press.

Strauss, C. (1992) Models and motives. In R. D'Andrade and C. Strauss (eds) *Human Motives and Cultural Models* (pp. 1–20). Cambridge: Cambridge University Press.

Suleri, S. (1992) *The Rhetoric of English India*. Chicago: Chicago University Press.

Street, B. (2002) Introduction. In Brian Street (ed.) *Literacy and Development: Ethnographic Perspectives* (pp. 1–17). London: Routledge

Swales, J. (1998) *Other Flooors, Other Voices*. Mahwah, NJ: Lawrence Erlbaum.

Thaker, P. (ed.) (1999) *English Reader: Standard 8*. Gandhinagar: Gujarat State Board of Textbooks.

Tollefson, J. and Tsui, A. (2004) *Medium of Instruction Policies: Which Agenda? Whose Agenda?* Mahwah, NJ: Lawrence Erlbaum.

Tharu, S., (ed.) (1997) *Subject to Change*. New Delhi: Orient Longman.

Tollefson, J. (ed.) (1995) *Power and Inequality in Language Education*. Cambridge: Cambridge University Press.

Tsoukas, H. (1998) Forms of knowledge and forms of life in organized contexts. In R. Chia (ed.) *In the Realm of Organization* (pp. 43–66). New York: Routledge.

Vaidik, V. (1973) *Angrezi hatao: kyon aur kaise? [Remove English How and Why?]*. Indore: All India Remove English Lobby.

Vamdatta, D., Joshi, P. and Patel, Y. (ed.) (2000) *English Reader: Standard 10*. Gandhinagar: Gujarat State Board of Textbooks.

Vidich, A. and Lyman, S. (1994) Qualitative methods: Their history in sociology and anthropology. In N. Denzin and Y. Lincoln (eds) *Handbook of Qualitative Research* (pp. 23–59). Thousand Oaks, CA: Sage.

Vishwanathan, G. (1989) *The Masks of Conquest: Literary Study and British Rule in India*. New York: Colombia University Press.

Waseem, M. (1995) Bhojpuri and the Eighth Schedule. In R. Gupta, A. Ami and K. Agarwal (eds) *Language and the State: Perspectives on The Eighth Schedule* (pp. 211–13). New Delhi: Creative Books.

Wartenberg, T. (1990) *The Forms of Power: From Domination to Transformation.* Philadelphia: Temple University Press.

Williams, R. (1977) *Marxism and Literature.* Oxford: Oxford University Press.

Wrong, D. (1979) *Power: Its Forms, Bases, and Uses.* New York: Harper and Row.

Index

Authors

Subjects